GOVERNMENT PROCEDURES AND OPERATIONS

INDEPENDENT REGULATORY COMMISSIONS

RULEMAKING AND COST-BENEFIT ANALYSIS ISSUES

GOVERNMENT PROCEDURES AND OPERATIONS

Additional books in this series can be found on Nova's website under the Series tab.

Additional E-books in this series can be found on Nova's website under the E-book tab.

GOVERNMENT PROCEDURES AND OPERATIONS

INDEPENDENT REGULATORY COMMISSIONS

RULEMAKING AND COST-BENEFIT ANALYSIS ISSUES

RUBEN MEIJER
EDITOR

Novinka
New York

For permission to use material from this book please contact us:
Telephone 631-231-7269; Fax 631-231-8175
Web Site: http://www.novapublishers.com

Library of Congress Cataloging-in-Publication Data

ISBN: 978-1-62808-103-9

Published by Nova Science Publishers, Inc. † New York

CONTENTS

PREFACE

Federal agencies regularly adopt rules, which have the force of law, to implement the statutes and programs authorized by Congress. Unless a statute directs otherwise, agencies generally must follow the requirements of the Administrative Procedure Act to promulgate rules. However, beginning with President Reagan, Presidents have maintained a centralized review process for "significant regulatory actions." Currently, Executive Order (EO) 12866, issued by President Clinton, imposes additional procedures agencies must follow before a rule can be finalized. This includes requiring agencies to submit proposed regulatory action to the Office of Information and Regulatory Affairs (OIRA) at the Office of Management and Budget (OMB) for review. Although EO 12866 applies to executive agencies, independent regulatory commissions (IRCs) are not required to submit their rules to OIRA for review. In the 112th Congress, Senator Rob Portman introduced S.3468, the Independent Regulatory Agency Analysis Act of 2012. Under this bill, the President could issue an executive order establishing centralized review procedures for IRCs. This book discusses the constitutionality and the legal effects of extending centralized review of rulemaking to IRCs.

Chapter 1 – Federal agencies regularly adopt rules, which have the force of law, to implement the statutes and programs authorized by Congress. Unless a statute directs otherwise, agencies generally must follow the requirements of the Administrative Procedure Act to promulgate rules. However, beginning with President Reagan, Presidents have maintained a centralized review process for "significant regulatory actions." Currently, Executive Order (EO) 12866, issued by President Clinton, imposes additional procedures agencies must follow before a rule can be finalized. This includes requiring agencies to submit proposed regulatory action to the Office of

Information and Regulatory Affairs (OIRA) at the Office of Management and Budget (OMB) for review. Although EO 12866 applies to executive agencies, independent regulatory commissions (IRC) are not required to submit their rules to OIRA for review. Debates have arisen among scholars and legislators as to whether the President has the authority to require both executive agencies and IRCs to submit their regulations for review by OIRA. In the 112th Congress, Senator Rob Portman introduced S. 3468, the Independent Regulatory Agency Analysis Act of 2012. Under this bill, the President could issue an executive order establishing centralized review procedures for IRCs. This report discusses the constitutionality and the legal effects of extending centralized review of rulemaking to IRCs.

Chapter 2 – When issuing regulations that have the full force and effect of law, agencies are required to follow certain procedures. The Administrative Procedure Act (APA) of 1946 set up the basic framework for rulemaking: agencies are required to publish a notice of rulemaking in the *Federal Register*, take comments on the proposed rule, and publish a final rule in the *Federal Register*. Since the passage of the APA, additional procedures have been established in various statutes, executive orders, and guidance documents.

One potential change to the rulemaking process that has been discussed over the past three decades and proposed in legislation in the 112th Congress is the extension of the requirements of Executive Order (E.O.) 12866 to the independent regulatory agencies, also known as independent regulatory commissions (hereafter referred to as IRCs). E.O. 12866 contains two major requirements: first, it requires that agencies complete cost-benefit analysis (CBA) of "economically significant" rules, considering the potential costs, benefits, and feasible alternatives to proposed and final rules. Second, the order requires centralized review of "significant" rules in the Office of Management and Budget's (OMB's) Office of Information and Regulatory Affairs (OIRA). Historically, the IRCs have been exempted from requirements for CBA and centralized review. Senator Rob Portman introduced a bill in the 112th Congress, S. 3468, that would authorize the President to extend to the IRCs, by executive order, E.O. 12866's requirements for CBA and OIRA review. If the requirements of E.O. 12866 were extended to the IRCs, there could be significant implications for those agencies.

Potential Extension of CBA Requirements. Proponents of extending the requirements argue that subjecting the IRCs to CBA requirements and OIRA review could improve the quality of regulations issued by those agencies. On the other hand, extending CBA requirements and OIRA review to the IRCs could grant OIRA (and by extension, the President) the potential authority to influence or delay rulemaking proceedings, and such a requirement could potentially decrease the independence of the IRCs. The IRCs with fewer regulatory responsibilities that issue relatively fewer "significant" rules each year may find the additional requirements of S. 3468 minimally burdensome, even if their current cost-benefit practices are not as rigorous as what would be required under E.O. 12866. Conversely, the IRCs with greater regulatory responsibilities or the IRCs with recently expanded regulatory responsibilities may find the additional CBA requirements more burdensome. It is also possible that some IRCs may not have the staff with the technical expertise necessary to conduct cost-benefit analysis that is more extensive than their current requirements.

Potential Extension of OIRA Review. The second major element of E.O. 12866 is OIRA review of "significant" regulations. During the review process, OIRA examines each regulation to ensure that the agency followed the principles and procedures outlined in E.O. 12866, including the applicable requirements for conducting CBA, and that the regulation is consistent with the policy preferences of the President. Numerous individuals, including former OIRA officials and several administrative law scholars, have spoken in support of potential OIRA review of regulations issued by IRCs. Much of this support for OIRA review relies on the underlying premise that increased presidential control, through OIRA review, of rulemaking could improve both the rulemaking process within agencies and the quality of the regulations themselves. On the other hand, some have expressed hesitation or opposition to the extension of OIRA review to the IRCs, suggesting that the independence of the IRCs could be compromised and that OIRA review of IRCs' rules could lead to delay.

Chapter 3 – Federal regulation, like taxing and spending, is one of the basic tools of government used to implement public policy. Although not as frequently examined as congressional or presidential policy making, the process of developing and framing rules is viewed by some as central to the definition and implementation of public policy in the United States. Regulations generally start with an act of Congress, and are the means by which statutes are implemented and specific requirements are established. The terms "rule" or "regulation" are often used interchangeably in discussions of the federal regulatory process. The Administrative Procedure Act of 1946 defines a *rule* as "the whole or part of an agency statement of general or particular applicability and future effect designed to implement, interpret, or prescribe law or policy." The procedures that federal agencies are required to follow in writing regulations are called the rulemaking process, and are the subject of this report.

During the past 60 to 65 years, Congress and various Presidents have developed an elaborate set of procedures and requirements to guide the federal rulemaking process, often with the implicit or explicit goal of reducing the amount of regulatory burden placed on the public. Statutory rulemaking requirements applicable to a wide range of agencies include the Administrative Procedure Act, the Regulatory Flexibility Act, the Paperwork Reduction Act, the Unfunded Mandates Reform Act, and the Information Quality Act. These and other cross-cutting rulemaking requirements often require some type of analysis on the part of the rulemaking agency before issuing a covered rule, but also often give agencies substantial discretion regarding whether the requirements are applicable. Other statutorily based rulemaking requirements are contained in agency- or program-specific laws, which provide varying levels of discretion regarding the substance of agencies' rules and may impose (or exclude) additional analytical or procedural requirements. The most important of the current set of presidential rulemaking requirements are in Executive Order 12866, which establishes presidential review of covered agencies' rulemaking within the Office of Management and Budget's Office of Information and Regulatory Affairs (OIRA). The executive order requires covered agencies to submit their significant rules to OIRA for review before they become final, and requires those rules to meet certain minimal standards. Other executive orders and presidential directives delineate other specific rulemaking requirements incumbent on covered agencies. However, these requirements also often provide substantial discretion to agencies regarding whether, and if so how, they are applied.

The purpose of this report is to provide Congress with an overview of the federal rulemaking process and a brief discussion of the major laws and executive orders that prescribe the procedures agencies are to apply when promulgating regulations.

In: Independent Regulatory Commissions
Editor: Ruben Meijer

ISBN: 978-1-62808-103-9

Chapter 1

PRESIDENTIAL REVIEW OF INDEPENDENT REGULATORY COMMISSION RULEMAKING: LEGAL ISSUES*

Vivian S. Chu and Daniel T. Shedd

SUMMARY

Federal agencies regularly adopt rules, which have the force of law, to implement the statutes and programs authorized by Congress. Unless a statute directs otherwise, agencies generally must follow the requirements of the Administrative Procedure Act to promulgate rules. However, beginning with President Reagan, Presidents have maintained a centralized review process for "significant regulatory actions." Currently, Executive Order (EO) 12866, issued by President Clinton, imposes additional procedures agencies must follow before a rule can be finalized. This includes requiring agencies to submit proposed regulatory action to the Office of Information and Regulatory Affairs (OIRA) at the Office of Management and Budget (OMB) for review. Although EO 12866 applies to executive agencies, independent regulatory commissions (IRC) are not required to submit their rules to OIRA for review. Debates have arisen among scholars and legislators as to whether the President has the authority to require both executive agencies and IRCs to submit their

* This is an edited, reformatted and augmented version of a Congressional Research Service publication, CRS Report for Congress R42720, prepared for Members and Committees of Congress, from www.crs.gov, dated November 28, 2012.

regulations for review by OIRA. In the 112th Congress, Senator Rob Portman introduced S. 3468, the Independent Regulatory Agency Analysis Act of 2012. Under this bill, the President could issue an executive order establishing centralized review procedures for IRCs. This report discusses the constitutionality and the legal effects of extending centralized review of rulemaking to IRCs.

INTRODUCTION

The Executive Branch has exercised control over agency rulemaking through executive orders such as Executive Order 12866.[1] This Executive Order requires executive agencies to submit significant rules to the Office of Information and Regulatory Affairs (OIRA) at the Office of Management and Budget (OMB) for review; however, it does not require the independent regulatory commissions (IRC) to comply with these requirements. This report discusses the constitutionality and the potential legal effects of extending centralized review of rulemaking to the IRCs.

OVERVIEW OF FEDERAL RULEMAKING

Federal agencies adopt rules to implement statutes that Congress has enacted.[2] These rules, although established by an administrative agency, maintain the force of law.[3] In order to be able to promulgate rules, Congress must grant that agency the power to do so through statute.[4] To control the process by which agencies create these rules, Congress has enacted statutes, such as the Administrative Procedure Act (APA),[5] that dictate what procedures an agency must follow to establish a final, legally binding rule.

Unless an agency's authorizing statute provides for different procedures, the APA provides the default practice that all agencies must follow in order to promulgate rules. The APA provides for both formal and informal rulemaking procedures.[6] The formal rulemaking procedures only need to be followed when an authorizing statute requires that a rulemaking proceed "on the record" after an opportunity for a hearing.[7] These formal rulemaking procedures are rare and most agencies follow the informal, "notice and comment" rulemaking procedures outlined in the APA and discussed below.[8]

Under informal rulemaking procedures, an agency must first publish a notice of proposed rulemaking (NPRM) in the *Federal Register*.[9] The NPRM must include "(1) a statement of the time, place, and nature of public rule making proceedings; (2) reference to the legal authority under which the rule is proposed; and (3) either the terms or substance of the proposed rule or a description of the subjects and issues involved."[10] After providing notice through the *Federal Register*, the agency must allow "interested persons an opportunity" to comment on the proposed rule.[11] Typically an agency will provide at least 30 days for public comment and this time period may be extended if the agency deems necessary.[12] After the comment period has ended, the agency is required to review the public comments and may then issue a final rule. When publishing the final rule in the *Federal Register*, the agency must provide a "concise general statement" of the rule's "basis and purpose."[13] The final rule may not go into effect until at least 30 days after it is published in the *Federal Register*, with certain exceptions.[14]

In addition to the APA, Congress has enacted numerous statutes that impose obligations on agencies when they engage in rulemaking procedures. Statutes such as the National Environmental Protection Act (NEPA),[15] the Regulatory Flexibility Act (RFA),[16] the Congressional Review Act (CRA),[17] and the Paperwork Reduction Act (PRA)[18] establish additional procedures and practices that the agencies must follow prior to establishing a finalized rule. Furthermore, the President has issued executive orders and guidance documents establishing additional requirements and procedures that agencies must follow before a rule can be finalized.

EXECUTIVE CONTROL OF AGENCY RULEMAKING

Numerous presidential administrations have attempted to maintain control over the agencies by establishing a centralized review process for certain agency rules.[19] Notably, President Reagan's issuance of Executive Order (EO) 12291 required agencies to have proposed and final rules reviewed by OMB prior to publication.[20] Upon election, President Clinton revised and replaced Reagan's order with EO 12866 but maintained the centralized review process for "significant regulatory actions."[21] Clinton's EO 12866 was maintained by both the George W. Bush and Obama Administrations and remains in force today.[22] When both the Reagan and Clinton Administrations issued their respective executive orders, they exempted statutorily-designated independent regulatory commissions (IRCs) from this centralized review process. Before discussing the requirements imposed by EO 12866, it is helpful to review briefly some of the features that make the IRCs generally insulated from presidential control.

What Are Independent Regulatory Commissions?

As mentioned, the centralized review portions of EO 12866 do not apply to the statutorily designated IRCs, also known as "independent regulatory agencies," identified in the PRA.[23] These IRCs share several traits that arguably insulate the agencies from the President's direct control. These characteristics include (1) "for cause" removal; (2) structural designs; (3) bypass of OMB legislative clearance; (4) bypass of OMB review of agency rulemaking; (5) bypass of OMB budget submissions; and (6) independent litigating authority.[24] For purposes of this report, we will only review the following traits—"for cause" removal, structural designs, and OMB bypass.

"For cause" Removal and Structural Design

"For cause" removal protection provides an element of insulation from presidential direction, as opposed to those officers who serve at the pleasure of the President and may be removed at will.[25] Typically, a removal provision may state that a member may be removed only "for cause" or for "inefficiency, neglect of duty, or malfeasance in office."[26]

Structural design also provides insulation from presidential control.[27] Congress has established numerous commissions with several members that serve "set terms expiring at staggered intervals, [and] who could be removed by the President only upon a showing of sufficient cause."[28] Other structural features may include an odd number of members of the commission, with no more than a simple majority appointed from one political party, who serve terms that tend to exceed the president's four-year term.[29] A bipartisan composition of a board and fixed terms set at staggered intervals attempt to create a collegial body that is insulated from outside political pressure.[30]

OMB Bypass (Legislative/ Rules/ Budget)

OMB acts as a coordination center for a variety of agency activities, which include reviewing legislative proposals and testimony to Congress;[31] overseeing agency rulemaking;[32] and approving budget requests.[33] The primary purpose of these OMB clearance procedures is to ensure that any legislative proposals, rules issued, or budgetary requests are consistent with the President's policies and programs.[34]

Despite OMB's coordinative and supervisory role, the IRCs may be exempted by statute or executive order from OMB clearance procedures, thereby providing these agencies with greater independence from the President. For instance, Congress exempts many of the financial regulatory agencies from submitting their legislative recommendations to any other agency prior to their submission to Congress "if such recommendation, [or] testimony ... include[s] a statement indicating that the views expressed ... are those of the agency ... and do not necessarily represent the views of the President."[35] As mentioned earlier, the IRCs are exempt from submitting their regulatory actions for OIRA review under EO 12866. Additionally, some of the IRCs, like the U.S. International Trade Commission (USITC) and Federal Communications Commission (FCC), are statutorily shielded from having their annual budget requests revised by OMB.[36]

Executive Order 12866

Executive Order 12866 (Executive Order or EO 12866) has numerous components,[37] one of which includes the establishment of "Centralized Review of Regulations" by OIRA within OMB.[38] Only executive agencies are subject to the centralized review of agency rulemaking provisions, while the IRCs have been exempt from this process.[39] The Executive Order defines an "agency" as "any authority of the United States that is an 'agency' under 44 U.S.C. § 3502(1), other than those considered to be independent regulatory agencies, as defined in [44 U.S.C. § 3502(5).]"[40] For purposes of this report, agencies to which centralized review applies shall be referred to as "executive agencies."

Section 6 of EO 12866, which establishes the centralized review process, requires an executive agency to submit to OIRA a list of its planned regulations and to identify all planned regulatory actions that the agency "believes are significant regulatory actions within the meaning of this Executive order." [41] The Executive Order defines "significant regulatory action" to be

> any regulatory action that is likely to result in a rule that may: (1) Have an annual effect on the economy of $100 million or more or adversely affect in a material way the economy, a sector of the economy, productivity, competition, jobs, the environment, public health or safety, or State, local, or tribal governments or communities; (2) Create a serious

inconsistency or otherwise interfere with an action taken or planned by another agency; (3) Materially alter the budgetary impact of entitlements, grants, user fees, or loan programs or the rights and obligations of recipients thereof; or (4) Raise novel legal or policy issues arising out of legal mandates, the President's priorities, or the principles set forth in this Executive order.[42]

OIRA, not the promulgating agency, makes the ultimate determination of whether a rule should be considered a "significant" rule.[43] Executive agencies must submit all planned regulations, whether they determine them to be significant or not, and OIRA will make its own determination within ten days of receiving the information on the proposed action.[44] All "significant regulatory actions" are subject to review by OIRA prior to their promulgation.

For any rulemaking that is deemed "significant," executive agencies must provide to OIRA the text of the regulation, a statement explaining the need for the regulation, an explanation of how the proposal will satisfy the need, and "an assessment of the potential costs and benefits of the regulatory action."[45] Additionally, executive agencies must also submit a statement establishing that the regulatory action is consistent with established law and the President's priorities without unduly interfering with state and local governments.[46]

Any rule that is determined to be "economically significant"[47] must meet further requirements. For these rules, executive agencies must provide a detailed cost-benefit analysis (CBA) of the proposed rule and must attempt to quantify those costs and benefits to the best of their ability.[48] They must also perform a CBA for any reasonable alternatives and provide "an explanation why the planned regulatory action is preferable to the identified potential alternatives."[49]

OIRA generally has 90 days to complete its review of the proposed agency action to ensure it comports with the principles of EO 12866.[50] An executive agency, to the extent permitted by law, is not allowed to finalize a rule by publishing it in the *Federal Register* until OIRA completes the review process.[51]

OIRA may return a proposed regulatory action to the executive agency "for further consideration" with an explanation detailing why OIRA believes the action fails to meet the requirements of EO 12866.[52] This may be because the executive agency failed to provide an adequate CBA or, in the case of an economically significant action, failed to adequately consider reasonable alternatives to the proposed action. Additionally, OIRA could return the regulation for further consideration if it feels that the proposed action may conflict with the President's priorities or an action already taken or planned by another agency. Upon return, the executive agency must then reconsider the rule and address OIRA's concerns before publishing the rule.[53] Any conflicts between OIRA and the executive agency are to be resolved by the President of the United States.[54]

Authority to Subject Agency Rulemakings to Centralized Review

Two factors have caused questions to arise when evaluating the President's authority to unilaterally require executive agencies to submit their rules to OIRA for review. First, Congress has delegated to the various executive agencies, not the President himself, the authority to implement federal programs through the creation of rules. Second, Congress has not by statute authorized the President to establish a centralized review of the rules agencies are statutorily authorized to promulgate. Given this, could the President be exceeding his constitutional authority by taking such action without direct approval from the legislative branch? Under what authority is the President taking such action?

One argument in support of the President's authority to require centralized review of agency rulemaking is the unitary executive theory.[55] This theory is based on the argument that the Founders vested all executive power in the President of the United States alone and gave him the power to "take Care that the Laws be faithfully executed."[56] Proponents of the unitary executive theory generally maintain that the President should thus have full control over the executive branch and should be able to direct officers in fulfilling their statutory obligations.[57] One proponent argues that "even if a statute grants discretion to the Secretary of State and explicitly prohibits presidential intervention in the decision-making process, the President retains the constitutional authority to substitute his own judgment for the Secretary's determination."[58] Proponents of a strong unitary executive theory, therefore, have little difficulty in justifying the constitutionality of a centralized review process. The Department of Justice (DOJ) Office of Legal Counsel (OLC) issued an opinion in support of the Reagan Administration's EO 12291 that draws from some of the same principles of the unitary executive theory while acknowledging certain limits to the President's authority over executive officers.[59]

The crux of OLC's argument rests on the President's constitutional power to "take Care that the Laws be faithfully executed."[60] The OLC opinion argues that the President's responsibility to ensure that all legislation is "faithfully executed" requires him to coordinate among the executive agencies as they implement a vast array of legislation through the rulemaking process.[61] The Supreme Court, in *Myers v. United States*, interpreted the Take Care Clause to mean that the President shall have the authority to "supervise and guide" the executive officers in the administration of the statutes to ensure "unitary and uniform execution of the laws."[62] By requiring the executive agencies to submit rules and CBAs for review,[63] OLC concludes that the President is only acting in a supervisory capacity to "take Care" that the laws are being faithfully executed. The opinion argues that EO 12291 does not exceed the President's Article II powers because he is not divesting the executive agencies of their statutory authority to exercise their congressionally delegated powers; he is merely ensuring that the executive agencies under his control are implementing their statutes in a uniform manner, consistent with the President's priorities. Moreover, when adhering to EO 12291 would conflict with statutory obligations, OLC notes that agencies are only required to comply with the Executive Order "to the extent permitted by law."

Another argument offered to support the President's authority to require centralized review of agency rulemaking is based on statutory interpretation, rather than a clear constitutional authority to take such action. An article by now Supreme Court Justice Elena Kagan, writing as a legal scholar, argues that Congress, when it delegates rulemaking authority to an executive agency in lieu of an IRC, has implicitly permitted the President to direct executive agency officials to reach certain conclusions.[64] Though Kagan contemplates a scenario in which the President orders an executive agency to reach a certain conclusion on an issue delegated to that agency, this authority to direct an agency official could likely justify the authority to subject those agency rules to centralized review.

Kagan's argument recognizes that Congress has the authority to limit the President's control over agency officials and their discretion to implement certain regulations. For instance, when Congress delegates decision-making authority to an IRC, the President may not interfere with the discretion given to that officer.[65] However, she argues that when Congress has delegated authority to an executive branch agency, and has not specifically limited the President's authority to control that agency decision, these statutes reflect congressional intent to permit the President to exercise control over that decision.[66] This is because Congress is well aware that executive officers are subordinate to the President, appointed by the President, removable by the President, and are otherwise subject to presidential oversight.[67] Furthermore, Congress knows how to isolate a specific decision from the President's influence—by delegating that decision to an IRC.[68] Therefore, she argues when Congress is silent, it is implicitly giving the President ultimate control over that legal authority. This control over agency decision making is likely sufficient to enable the President to require OIRA review of executive agency rules and to resolve any disputes between OIRA and the agency.

Another approach to examine the President's authority over executive agencies is by evaluating these executive orders under the tripartite framework from Justice Jackson's concurring opinion in *Youngstown Sheet & Tube Co. v. Sawyer*.[69] Justice Jackson's concurring opinion set forth three types of circumstances in which presidential authority may be asserted and established a scheme for analyzing the validity of presidential actions in relation to constitutional and congressional authority.[70] First, if the President has acted according to an express or implied grant of congressional authority, presidential "authority is at its maximum."[71] Second, in situations where Congress has neither granted nor denied authority to the President, the President acts in reliance only "upon his own independent powers, but there is a zone of twilight in which he and Congress may have concurrent authority, or in which its distribution is uncertain."[72] Third, in instances where presidential action is "incompatible with the express or implied will of Congress," the power of the President is at its minimum.[73] In such a circumstance, presidential action must rest upon an exclusive Article II power.[74]

An argument could be made that the issuance of executive orders requiring OIRA review of executive agency rules is an action that falls within Jackson's second prong—the "zone of twilight." Congress has never given the President express authority to require centralized review of agency rules.[75] Additionally, Congress has never expressly denied the President the authority to establish such requirements. Therefore, under this argument, the President's authority to act by executive order would be placed in category two's "zone of twilight." Justice Jackson's opinion declared there are no specific rules to determine whether an action in this category is constitutional, but notes that the validity of the action will likely "depend on the imperatives of events and contemporary imponderables rather than on abstract theories of law."[76] Justice Jackson's opinion seems to suggest that practical considerations should be evaluated when determining the scope of presidential authority to act in the "zone of twilight." It could be argued that evaluating the orders based on these practical considerations would lend support for the President's authority to issue such orders, given the seemingly general support for centralized review,[77] the complex nature of the administrative state that must be coordinated,[78] and Congress's apparent acquiescence on the issue.[79]

In contrast, others have argued that the President's imposition of centralized review without congressional authorization runs afoul of the separation of powers under the tripartite framework.[80] This argument notes that Congress has not delegated by statute, impliedly or expressly, the authority to require a centralized review of agency rules. In fact, the argument posits that Congress has impliedly *denied* the President the authority to assume this type of control over the rulemaking process. Congress's expansive use of the legislative veto,[81] early congressional responses to President Nixon's attempts to make policy through the OMB budget process, and congressional rejection of legislative proposals to create a central office to evaluate agency performance all may be viewed as actions taken by Congress to limit the President's authority in the sphere of agency policymaking.[82] Following this approach, the President is viewed as acting in the third category under Justice Jackson's opinion from *Youngstown.* Under this argument, in order for the President's centralized review requirements to be constitutional, the President must be able to rely solely on his own Article II powers.

Although unitary executive proponents, discussed above, argue that the President has the requisite authority to impose centralized review based solely on his Article II powers, some scholars argue that the Vesting Clause and Take Care Clause, discussed above, do not grant the President a broad power, but rather show that the President is intended to be an "agent of Congress," carrying out the legislative will.[83] Opponents of the unitary executive theory note that the authority to "take Care" that the laws be executed does not imply the authority to execute them himself.[84] Rather, when Congress delegates to a subordinate official, the subordinate official has ultimate control over the decision and the President must "take Care" that only that official exercises the delegated authority. If it were true that the President is acting within Justice Jackson's third category with his powers at a minimum, these powers could arguably not be enough to sustain the constitutionality of the executive orders. These executive orders requiring agencies to submit their regulations for presidential review, it may be argued, impermissibly interfere with Congress's delegation of authority to the specific agency and could be potentially struck down for unconstitutionally breaching Congress's powers.[85]

Debates about the constitutionality of these executive orders have mostly receded since their initial issuance. Most scholars and organizations now seem to agree that the President has the authority to conduct centralized review of the executive agency rulemaking process.[86] One author notes that "the once rather vibrant legal and policy debate over the pros and cons of presidential review has gradually evolved into a fairly broad agreement that it is not only legal, but that if properly administered, it is essential to effective executive branch management."[87] Presidential review of agency rulemaking has existed in some form since 1971 and the authority has been exercised under EO 12866 for nearly twenty years without any action from Congress to restrain the process. The implicit acquiescence of both Congress and the courts regarding the constitutionality of these orders appears to provide practical support for the proposition that the President has the authority to exercise centralized control over the executive agencies.

Furthermore, although no courts have directly decided the constitutional validity of these executive orders,[88] cases dealing with the President's authority to consult and advise his executive officers could arguably be viewed as offering support for the constitutional validity of centralized review. The U.S. Court of Appeals for the D.C. Circuit (DC Circuit), when determining whether the President could consult nonpublicly with his EPA Administrator regarding a proposed rule, stated

> The authority of the President to control and supervise executive policymaking is derived from the Constitution; the desirability of such control is demonstrable from the practical realities of administrative rulemaking. Regulations such as those involved here demand a careful weighing of cost, environmental, and energy considerations. They also have broad implications for national economic policy. Our form of government simply could not function effectively or rationally if key executive policymakers were isolated from each other and from the Chief Executive.[89]

This statement from the DC Circuit could be viewed as lending support to the principles outlined in the 1981 OLC opinion. The court notes that the President may "control and supervise executive policymaking,"[90] and appears to indicate that, in the complex realm of administrative law, effective coordination between the executive agencies and the President is arguably necessary if not desirable.

Further questions, however, could arise regarding whether the President could extend this review to cover the IRCs. The following sections discuss whether the President has the constitutional authority to require centralized review of the IRCs' rulemakings or whether these IRCs must remain free from this type of executive influence.

INDEPENDENT REGULATORY COMMISSIONS AND OIRA REVIEW

Although many groups and scholars have called for the extension of centralized review to the IRCs, this extension has not yet occurred.[91] The following section addresses whether the President has sufficient legal authority to extend such requirements to the IRCs, assuming there are adequate legal grounds for general OIRA review of agency rulemaking (described above).

President's Authority for Extending OIRA Review to the IRCs

Although bypassing OMB review is a hallmark trait of agency independence, prior presidential administrations have considered subjecting the IRCs to OIRA review.[92] Both Presidents Reagan and Clinton obtained legal opinions from OLC, which concluded there is sufficient legal basis to apply the centralized review requirements to the IRCs.[93] Determinations not to extend the CBA requirements to the IRCs were apparently due to political rather than legal impediments. Yet, S. 3468, a bill introduced by Senator Rob Portman in the 112th Congress, would provide that: "The President may by Executive order require an independent regulatory agency to comply, to the extent permitted by law," with the centralized review requirements that are applicable to other executive agencies. While the stated purpose of this bill is to affirm the President's existing constitutional authority to take such action, as will be discussed below, the introduction of this proposal has also brought renewed attention to lingering questions regarding whether the President has the legal authority to extend requirements of the executive order to the IRCs without such congressional action.

When President Reagan issued EO 12291 in 1981, both support and concern over the constitutionality of OMB's role in the administrative process had been expressed.[94] The same arguments made in the 1981 OLC opinion in support of the constitutionality to conduct centralized review of regulations via executive order, discussed above, could also apply in extending the review requirements of EO 12866 to the IRCs. Relying on the *Myers* decision to reach its conclusion, [95] OLC states it is "unclear to what extent Congress may insulate [non-independent] executive agencies from presidential supervision," given that the Court in *Myers* held that the President had an illimitable power of removal over "purely executive officers."[96] While OLC applies *Myers* to explain the President's supervisory role over agencies whose heads are removable by the President at will,[97] the Supreme Court's decision in *Humphrey's Executor v. United States* would likely provide guidance over whether the President may perform the same supervisory role with respect to agencies whose heads are restricted to removal "for cause."[98]

In *Humphrey's Executor*, the Court unanimously upheld the Federal Trade Commission (FTC) Act, which restricted the President's ability to remove an agency official.[99] Specifically, the President could remove an FTC commissioner only on the basis of "inefficiency, neglect of duty, or malfeasance in office."[100] Notably, the Court also pronounced in dicta that the congressional intent in creating the FTC was to create a body "independent of executive authority *except in its selection* [of commissioners]."[101] A separate OLC opinion, which discussed the application of EO 12291 to the IRCs, wrestles with this characterization of the FTC, as it serves as a model for many of the IRCs.[102] OLC lists several reasons why the dicta would not control whether the President has authority to supervise the IRCs in rulemaking. Among these reasons, OLC contends that insulation from the President for purposes of agency adjudication was not "pertinent to supervision of rulemaking,"[103] and the Court had not considered that "Executive Branch and independent agencies engage in rulemaking in a functionally indistinguishable fashion."[104] It also underscores the President's other statutory powers over the IRCs, which "recognize the legitimacy of some presidential influence in the activities of independent agencies ... "105 Although *Humphrey's Executor* affirmed congressional intent to minimize presidential supervision of the IRCs, OLC ultimately concludes this does not prevent the President from "supervis[ing] [the IRCs] as necessary to ensure that they are faithfully executing the laws, although [the President] may not displace their substantive discretion to decide particular adjudicative or rulemaking matters."[106]

The OLC argument in favor of presidential supervision over the administrative process appears to draw from the principles which are at the root of the unitary executive doctrine.[107] Under this view, despite the intent to have an agency insulated from presidential control, the "Constitution makes no provision for a category of agencies existing 'outside' the executive, legislative, and judicial branches. The President is the constitutionally specified agency of the Congress in implementation of federal law." [108] Put another way, the "law that delegates authority to an independent regulatory commission, like the law that places final decision in the hands of cabinet officials, is constitutional and thus part of the body of law to the faithful execution of which the President is obliged to see."[109]

A statutory approach could also be taken in examining whether the President has authority to include the IRCs within EO 12866. The terms of removal of executive officers may assist in analyzing if Congress has granted authority to the President to supervise the IRCs, which informs whether these agencies may be subject to review requirements via executive order.[110] Although there are no definitions for these removal terms, see discussion *infra*, a narrow interpretation of removal would mean the President is limited to firing the IRC heads for reasons unrelated to policy—that is, "the President may discharge people for corruption ('malfeasance in office'), for refusing to do their jobs ('neglect of duty'), or for more general dereliction in the sense of gross incompetence ... ('inefficiency')."[111] This interpretation would likely preclude the President from supervising an IRC's policy choices, such that he would have little authority to extend the Executive Order.[112] A broad interpretation of the terms, on the other hand, would mean the President could remove an agency member "for any number of actual or perceived transgressions" of presidential will.[113] Under this interpretation, the President could have a "high degree of authority over the policy choices of independent agencies," in which case "inclusion of [the IRCs] within the executive order is plainly lawful, simply as a statutory matter."[114]

Alternatively, at least one scholar suggests that the Court's latest removal decision in *Morrison v. Olson*,[115] potentially offers new guidance on the scope of the President's supervisory powers.[116] After *Morrison*, the modified test on the constitutionality of a statutory removal restriction is whether the law "impedes the President's ability to perform his constitutional duty."[117] This shift demonstrates the Court "moving away from loose conceptions that whole agencies have a special constitutional status outside the executive branch, and toward a more focused inquiry whether the President has been denied a supervisory role that is appropriate to the particular function involved."[118] Accordingly, rather than examining whether the President could extend executive order requirements to the IRCs as whole, the new inquiry would be "whether the executive's accountability can be trusted" and "whether political accountability would interfere with successful performance of the function."[119] This would involve identifying rulemaking programs on a case-by-case basis to determine whether the President may supervise agency rulemaking.

The legal arguments against application of EO 12866 to executive agencies, discussed above, would also apply to the IRCs. However, while an analysis under Justice Jackson's concurrence from *Youngstown* could lead to the conclusion that coordinating regulatory review of executive agencies by executive order would not violate separation of powers principles,[120] the outcome could be different when applying the tripartite framework to the IRCs. The third prong of the framework states that where presidential action is "incompatible with the express or implied will of Congress," the power of the President is at its minimum.[121]

There is no express congressional prohibition on the President conducting centralized review on executive agencies or the IRCs. However, the question with respect to the IRCs is whether an inference may be drawn that it is the "implied will of Congress" the President refrain from a supervisory role over the IRCs, based on congressional intent to insulate the IRCs, as well as statutory provisions that secure OMB bypass or presidential bypass for some IRCs.[122] If such were the case, the presidential action must rest upon an exclusive power.[123] This would likely call into question whether it would be sufficient for the President take such action by relying solely on the general authority vested to him as head of the executive branch, and his authority to "take Care" the laws be executed faithfully.[124] Notably, if S. 3468 were to become law, the first prong under *Youngstown* would likely be satisfied. As the President would be extending the Executive Order pursuant to an express grant of congressional authority, it is likely there would be little question that such action was valid.

Recourse for IRC Noncompliance

If the President were to amend EO 12866 to include the IRCs, this raises the question of what types of action may be taken to enforce agency compliance. If an agency disregarded the Executive Order, could the President fire a member of an IRC, who has "for cause" removal protection? Or, could action be taken through the courts to enforce compliance? Alternatively, Congress could codify the provisions of EO 12866, which has been previously considered.[125]

A statute mandating compliance with the OIRA review process could affect the recourse available to the President and the availability of judicial review.

President's Recourse

Through OMB, the President arguably plays a purely supervisory role over the administrative process, with no authority to determine the outcomes of the agency's final judgment.[126] It is therefore plausible that an agency could disregard an OIRA request to defer rulemaking or to reassess a proposed rule for lack of adequate CBA. In this situation, the only recourse within the President's control for agency noncompliance would be to remove the head of the agency, as he or she serves at the pleasure of the President.[127] However, if an IRC were to disregard the OMB process, the question arises as to whether the President has grounds to remove the members of the agency if they have "for cause" removal protection. This, in turn, depends on what it means to be removed "for cause." Before proceeding to discuss the potential meaning of "for cause" removal, we must first discuss whether "for cause" removal applies to members of an IRC where the establishing statute is silent on removal.

Does "for cause" Removal Protection Apply to Members of the IRCs if the Statute Is Silent?

In the context of removal under the Appointments Clause,[128] the Supreme Court has declared as a general matter: "[i]n the absence of a specific provision to the contrary, the power of removal is incident to the power of appointment."[129] Under this principle, the presumption is if a statute is silent on removal, the appointing authority has the power to remove, unless prevented by law. Although a majority of the IRCs have explicit provisions in their statutes providing that members may be removed only "for cause"[130] or "for inefficiency, neglect of duty, or malfeasance in office,"[131] some are silent on removal. These include, among others, the Securities and Exchange Commission (SEC), the National Credit Union Administration (NCUA), and the Federal Election Commission (FEC).[132] Statutory silence on removal may raise the issue of whether members of these agencies may be removed only "for cause." For at these three agencies—the SEC, NCUA, and FEC—lower courts have inferred the application of a "for cause" removal restriction.

In *Wiener v. United States*, the Supreme Court addressed whether President Eisenhower could remove a member of the War Claims Commission (WCC) despite the statute's silence on removal.[133] Reviewing the legislative history of the War Claims Act of 1948[134] as well as the distinctive adjudicatory functions of the WCC,[135] the Court concluded the President could not remove the member at will.[136] It found many similarities between the

WCC and the FTC, whose restriction on removal had been upheld in *Humphrey's Executor*. After likening the structure, functions, and purpose of the WCC to the FTC—that is, the quasi-judicial functions of the WCC, and the congressional intent the WCC to be "free from control or coercive influence"[137]—the Court was "compelled to conclude that no such power [of at will removal] ... is impliedly conferred upon by statute simply because Congress said nothing about it."[138]

Subsequent courts that have also read into an otherwise silent statute a "for cause" removal restriction have generally followed the Court's approach in *Wiener*.[139] In *Swan v. Clinton*, the DC Circuit reviewed the NCUA's "function, statutory language and legislative history" to determine whether its Board members enjoy removal protection during their appointed terms.[140] The DC Circuit held that it would assume that Board members have removal protection during their appointed terms, because the legislative background was not so "ambiguous as not to permit us to discount the possibility that Congress did intend at least [removal protection during the] term."[141] Similarly, in *SEC v. Blinder*, the federal court of appeals reviewed the structural design, as well as the nature of the SEC's functions (quasi-legislative/judicial), and found that it could assume, without deciding, that SEC commissioners, like the FTC commissioners in *Humphrey's Executor*, may be removed only for "inefficiency, neglect of duty, or malfeasance in office."[142] The DC Circuit likewise found the FEC to be "patterned on the classic independent regulatory agency sanctioned ... in *Humphrey's Executor*" in which case it held that it could "safely assume that the President would at minimum have authority to discharge a commissioner for good cause—if for no other."[143]

Although the holding in *Wiener* could apply broadly to the IRCs whose statutes are silent on removal, it is likely a court would act like the DC Circuit in *Swan* and review each of these commissions on a case-by-case basis to determine whether a "for cause" limitation on removal can be read into the establishing statute.[144] However, it may be likely that the IRCs without an explicit removal provision and that are exempt from EO 12866[145] may be more similar to the FTC and WCC, such that a reviewing court would apply the rationale in *Wiener*, and a "for cause" removal restriction could be read into their statutes. As "for cause" removal protection applies to many of the IRCs by statute, and assuming that a "for cause" provision can be read into the statute of other IRCs, the next issue raised is whether noncompliance with the requirements of EO 12866 would be grounds upon which agency members may be removed "for cause."

Does Noncompliance with an Executive Order Give Rise to "for cause" Removal?

There does not appear to have been an occasion where the President has successfully removed, on an involuntary basis, an individual with "for cause" removal protection.[146] Moreover, it remains unclear as to the type of conduct that could give rise to removal under such circumstances, as these terms have not been defined by statute or the courts.[147] For example, in *Humphrey's Executor*, President Franklin Roosevelt had asked a Commissioner of the FTC for his resignation stating, "I do not feel that your mind and my mind go along together on either the policies or the administering of the Federal Trade Commission."[148] The Commissioner declined to resign, and the President notified him that he was removed from office. The Court stated that "the intent of the [FTC] act is to limit the executive power of removal to the causes enumerated, the existence of none of which is claimed here."[149] This case provides a sense of the type of conduct that would not provide grounds for removal within a "for cause" standard. Although the Court refrained from defining the removal terms, its conclusion appears to indicate that merely holding political views that differ from the President does not constitute grounds upon which the President may remove an individual "for cause." Notably, both Congress and DOJ also have opined on the meaning of "good cause" in the context of the Independent Counsel position, at issue in *Morrison v. Olson*. From DOJ's point of view, removal for "good cause" could exist if an independent counsel "refused to obey a presidential order to grant immunity to the target of an investigation."[150] The Senate rejected this interpretation, stating the removal protection was for the purpose of preventing the firing of an official "unless he or she engages in some type of misconduct [such as] taking a bribe or committing an impropriety."[151] This coupled with the Court's decisions in *Humphrey's Executor* and *Wiener* where the Court indicated that removal had to involve the "rectitude" of the government official could signify a more limited ability of the President to fire agency heads with "for cause" removal protection.[152]

On the other hand, the Court in *Bowsher v. Synar* noted that the applicable statute conferred "very broad" removal power upon Congress, whereby the Comptroller General could be removed for "any number of actual or perceived transgressions of legislative will."[153] Legal scholars have suggested that "for cause" provisions could be interpreted broadly so the President may remove an IRC member "under a broad array of circumstances, including a commissioner's frequent or important failure to follow the President's wishes with respect to what is required by sound policy."[154] In addition, this could include removal of an IRC head for refusing to follow certain presidential directives, such as an order to conduct CBA of a proposed regulation.[155]

The parameters for the conduct which give rise to removal "for cause" will remain less than clear, absent guidance by the courts or Congress. Were an IRC to disregard a presidential directive to follow OIRA review on proposed regulation, it appears uncertain whether this would constitute grounds by which the President could remove a member of an IRC "for cause." Thus, the President may have little or limited recourse to enforce an IRC's compliance with the Executive Order. Notably, S. 3468, as discussed above, would not require the IRCs to comply with EO 12866 by statute; rather, the bill would authorize the President to require such conduct by executive order. The bill does not address whether noncompliance could constitute grounds for removal. It only requires the head of the agency, who does not comply with the executive order, to submit explanations of noncompliance with the proposed and final significant rule.[156] Thus, even if S. 3468 became law and the President chose to extend to centralized review requirements to the IRCs, the President would face the same limits on enforcing IRC compliance, given the uncertainties of what constitutes "for cause" removal.

Were Congress to codify the statutory provisions of EO 12866 such that the IRCs are mandated to comply with the centralized review procedures, it may still remain unclear whether noncompliance with a statute would give the President "cause" to fire an agency head. As discussed, it is uncertain what conduct permits the President to remove an official "for cause." Although it is less clear whether noncompliance with an executive order would be grounds for removal under a "for cause" standard, a persuasive argument could be made that noncompliance with a statute rises to the level of removal "for cause." A reviewing court may find that failing to comply with a statutory directive more clearly constitutes "neglect of duty" or "malfeasance of office."

Judicial Recourse

In addition to the recourse available to the President, discussed above, individuals could challenge the validity of an agency rule if the agency fails to comply with the requirements of centralized review. However, due to restrictions on judicial review contained in EO 12866, judicial review would only be available if Congress, through statute, permitted the courts to hear cases regarding compliance with centralized review requirements. The following sections discuss the limitations on judicial review contained in EO

12866 and the potential for judicial review if Congress authorizes the courts to hear challenges.

Executive Order 12866 Restricts Judicial Review

Although compliance with rulemaking procedure requirements that are established by statute are often subject to judicial review,[157] the final section of EO 12866 provides that there shall be no judicial review for agency compliance with the order. Section 10 of Executive Order 12866 declares:

> Nothing in this Executive order shall affect any otherwise available judicial review of agency action. This Executive order is intended only to improve the internal management of the Federal Government and does not create any right or benefit, substantive or procedural, enforceable at law or equity by a party against the United States, its agencies or instrumentalities, its officers or employees, or any other person.

Therefore, no individual may question the validity of an agency action for noncompliance with the centralized review procedures set forth by EO 12866. If the President were to extend the centralized review of rulemaking to the IRCs, it seems clear that the preclusion of judicial review would also extend to these IRCs.

Courts have ruled that EO 12866 and its predecessor orders have effectively removed questions regarding compliance with the order from judicial scrutiny. In 2009, the United States Tax Court held that EO 12866 precluded a challenge to whether a regulation was actually a "significant regulatory action" requiring review by OIRA.[158]

In that case, the petitioner argued that the IRS violated EO 12866 when the agency failed to identify the challenged temporary income tax regulation as a "significant regulatory action" and submit it to OIRA for review.[159] However, the court quoted § 10 of EO 12866 and dismissed the argument swiftly by stating "petitioner has no right to challenge compliance with Executive Order 12866."[160]

Similarly, in an earlier case that involved Reagan's EO 12291, the U.S. Court of Appeals for the Sixth Circuit ruled that the order's provisions precluding judicial review established that no challenge could be made against an agency for noncompliance.[161] From these decisions, it seems to be well established that § 10 of EO 12866 effectively precludes judicial review of compliance with the order.[162]

Judicial Recourse for Noncompliance with Statute

Although EO 12866 precludes judicial review, Congress could enact a statute that would require agencies, both executive agencies and the IRCs, to comport with centralized review and subject their compliance to judicial scrutiny. If compliance with the centralized review process were to be subject to judicial review, what effect would this have on the IRCs and executive agencies?

Review of agency actions for compliance with the centralized review process, such as performing an adequate CBA, would provide courts with another avenue to set aside or vacate a rule for failure to comply with rulemaking procedures. If an agency failed to follow the statutorily imposed review requirements, claims could be brought under the APA challenging agency actions as arbitrary or capricious or otherwise not in compliance with the law.[163] Existing decisions can provide an illustration for how agencies might be held to comply with CBA requirements. The remainder of this section discusses cases brought against the SEC for failure to consider the costs and benefits of their regulatory actions.

Although the IRCs are not subject to the OIRA review process, many of them are required to consider the costs and benefits of their rules. However, such obligations are not imposed by executive order, but rather by statute. For example, the Investment Company Act (ICA) obligates the SEC to consider the economic effects of a new rule.[164] If the SEC promulgates a rule without adequately assessing the economic impacts, a court can vacate the rule as an arbitrary or capricious action under the APA.[165] Thus, when courts are permitted to review the economic analyses of an agency, the imposition of the agency's rules may be delayed by possible court action.

The DC Circuit has vacated SEC rules and remanded rules back to the Commission for further consideration. The court has taken such action for the agency's failure to adequately consider the costs imposed by a rule, failure to consider possible alternatives to a rule, and for relying on insufficient data or unpersuasive studies. In 2005, the DC Circuit remanded to the SEC for further consideration a rule that required mutual funds to have independent directors represent at least 75% of the board of directors in order to qualify for certain exemptions.[166] The court held that, in promulgating the rule, the SEC did not adequately consider the costs that would be imposed on mutual funds. The SEC argued that there was no "reliable basis for determining" how mutual funds would seek to comply with the requirement, and therefore it could not easily determine the potential costs.[167] The court noted that this did not relieve the SEC from its obligation to estimate, as best it could, the economic impact of the new requirement. The court held that the lack of an economic impact analysis violated the SEC's obligations under the ICA and APA.[168] Furthermore, the court determined that the SEC had also failed to adequately consider alternatives to their promulgated rule, in violation of the APA. Although the SEC is not required to consider every possible alternative, the court noted that two dissenting Commissioners from the SEC raised the possible alternative and that it warranted adequate consideration.[169]

In 2011, in *Business Roundtable v. SEC*,[170] the DC Circuit vacated another SEC rule, which would have required public companies to disclose information to shareholders regarding shareholder-nominated candidates for board of director positions. The court again noted that, pursuant to the ICA, the SEC had an obligation to "determine as best it can the economic implications of the rule."[171] The court found numerous problems with the SEC's justifications for the rule and determined, among other things, that the Commission: relied on "relatively unpersuasive studies" while dismissing other studies; "discounted the costs ... but not the benefits" of the new rule; and established the rule without obtaining important data relating to the frequency of election contests.[172] It determined the SEC's action to be arbitrary and capricious under the APA and vacated the rule.[173]

These cases illustrate that allowing a court to review an IRC's or executive agency's rule for compliance with centralized review requirements, such as performing an adequate CBA, could provide another tool for vacating or delaying the rule. If Congress considers subjecting agencies to such judicial review, it likely would be important for Congress to evaluate the potential policy and institutional implications as there could be more legal challenges to agency rules.

CONCLUSION

Federal agencies regularly adopt rules pursuant to the APA, which have the force of law, to implement the statutes and programs authorized by Congress. Beginning with President Reagan and continued by President Clinton, the executive branch, through OIRA, has maintained a centralized review process for "significant regulatory actions." The provisions of EO 12866 establish additional steps that executive agencies must follow before a rule can be finalized. Although debate surrounded whether the President has the authority to impose these procedural obligations on executive agencies, there seems to be fairly broad agreement that he has adequate legal grounds for doing so. IRCs, however, are exempt from EO 12866, but there has been consideration of extending these executive requirements to encompass the IRCs. Drawing from principles of the unitary executive, arguments have been made in favor of the President's authority to include IRCs in the OIRA review process as it is part of his constitutional authority to "take Care" that the laws are faithfully executed. Others, however, argue that the President does not have legal authority to act because Congress has not authorized this process and such action would be in contravention to Congress's implied will, as arguably evident by other statutes, to insulate the IRCs from presidential control.

However, were the President to extend EO 12866 to include the IRCs or were the Congress to codify the provisions of the Executive Order, questions arise as to the President's, as well as the courts', ability to enforce compliance. The President's direct recourse to take action against an IRC that disregards the Executive Order may be limited because members of the IRCs typically enjoy "for cause" removal protection. As the meaning of "for cause" has not been defined by Congress or the courts, it is unclear what conduct may permit the President to remove an IRC member. This may still be the case even if the provisions of EO 12866 were codified, although failure to follow a statutory requirement could be more credible grounds for removing a member of an IRC with "cause." Courts are unlikely to grant judicial review for an IRC's failure to comply with EO 12866, as there is a provision that expressly precludes judicial review for noncompliance. However, were judicial review provided via statute, claims could be brought against the IRCs under the APA challenging agency actions as arbitrary or capricious or otherwise not in compliance with the law.

End Notes

[1] Exec. Order No. 12866, 58 Fed. Reg. 51,735 (Sept. 30, 1993).

[2] For more information on the rulemaking process, see CRS Report R41546, A Brief Overview of Rulemaking and Judicial Review, by Todd Garvey and Daniel T. Shedd; CRS Report RL32240, The Federal Rulemaking Process: An Overview, coordinated by Maeve P. Carey.

[3] Chrysler Corp. v. Brown, 441 U.S. 281, 295 (1979).

[4] See Brannan v. Stark, 342 U.S. 451, 462-65 (1952).

[5] Administrative Procedure Act of 1946, Pub. L. No. 79-404, 60 Stat. 237 (1946) (codified as amended at 5 U.S.C. §§ 551 et seq.).

[6] See 5 U.S.C. §§ 553, 556-57.

[7] 5 U.S.C. § 553.

[8] Id.

[9] 5 U.S.C. § 553(b). The APA provides an exception from notice or hearing if the agency has "good cause." Id.

[10] Id.

[11] 5 U.S.C. § 553(c).

[12] The APA does not mandate a minimum time for comments.

[13] Id.

[14] 5 U.S.C. § 553(d). The APA provides an exception from the 30 day rule if the agency has "good cause." Id.

[15] 42 U.S.C. §§ 4321-4347 (requiring agencies to take into consideration the environmental impacts of major federal actions).

[16] 5 U.S.C. §§ 601-612 (requiring agencies to consider the impact of regulations on "small entities").

[17] 5 U.S.C. §§ 801-808 (requiring agencies to submit rules to Congress for congressional review of the proposed rules).

[18] 44 U.S.C. §§ 3501-3520 (requiring OMB approval when an agency seeks to collect information from an outside party).

[19] In 1971 President Nixon issued a "Quality of Life Review" program requiring agencies to submit certain proposed and final rules to OMB for review. See Angel Manual Moreno, Presidential Coordination of the Independent Regulatory Process, 8 Admin L.J. Am. U. 461, 494-96 (1994).

[20] Exec. Order No. 12291, 3 C.F.R. § 127 (1981 compilation).

[21] Exec. Order No. 12866, 58 Fed. Reg. 51,735 (Sept. 30, 1993). The definition of "significant regulatory action" is defined infra in the discussion on "Executive Order 12866."

[22] President George W. Bush issued EO 13258 and EO 13422, making technical amendments to EO 12866, but otherwise maintained the centralized review requirements from EO 12866. Exec. Order No. 13258, 67 Fed. Reg. 9385 (Feb. 28, 2002); Exec. Order No. 13422, 72 Fed. Reg. 2763 (Jan. 23, 2007) (revoked by Exec. Order No. 13497, 74 Fed. Reg. 6113 (Feb. 4, 2009). Most recently, President Obama issued EO 13563, essentially reaffirming the requirements and duties outlined in EO 12866. Exec. Order No. 13563, 76 Fed. Reg. 3821 (Jan. 18, 2011).

[23] 44 U.S.C. §§ 3501 et seq. The "independent regulatory agencies" identified in the PRA, which are exempt from some requirements of the act, are: the Board of Governors of the Federal Reserve System (Federal Reserve), the Commodity Futures Trading Commission (CFTC), the Consumer Product Safety Commission (CPSC), the Federal Communications Commission (FCC), the Federal Deposit Insurance Commission (FDIC), the Federal Energy Regulatory Commission (FERC), the Federal Housing Finance Authority (FHFA), the Federal Maritime Commission (FMC), the Federal Trade Commission (FTC), the Interstate Commerce Commission (ICC), the Mine Enforcement Safety and Health Review Commission (MESHRA), the National Labor Relations Board (NLRB), the Nuclear Regulatory Commission (NRC), the Occupational Safety and Health Review Commission (OSHRC), the Postal Regulatory Commission (PRC), the Securities and Exchange Commission (SEC), the Bureau of Consumer Financial Protection (CFPB), the Office of Financial Research, the Office of the Comptroller of the Currency, and any other similar agency designated by statute as a Federal independent regulatory agency or commission. Id. at § 3502(5). Though not listed, the U.S. International Trade Commission (USITC) is considered to be a part of this list, falling into the last category. See 19 U.S.C. § 1330(f) (stating that the U.S. International Trade Commission "shall be considered to be an independent regulatory agency for purposes of chapter 35 of title 44").

[24] See, e.g., Marshall J. Breger and Gary J. Edles, Established by Practice: The Theory and Operation of Independent Federal Agencies, 52 Admin. L. Rev. 1111 (2000), and Paul R. Verkuil, Symposium: The Independence of Independent Agencies: The Purposes and Limits of Independent Agencies, 37 Duke L.J. 257, 262-63 (1988). See also Free Enterprise Fund v. Public Company Accounting Oversight Board, 561 U.S. __; 130 S. Ct. 3138 (2010) [hereinafter PCAOB]. These traits have been used to identify other agencies, like the Social Security Administration, that are considered independent from the President, but that have not been designated as an IRC under 42 U.S.C. § 3502(5).

[25] See Brett M. Kavanaugh, Article: Separation of Powers During the Forty Fourth Presidency and Beyond, 93 Minn. L. Rev. 1454, 1471-72 (2009).

[26] 12 U.S.C. § 242 (Federal Reserve) ("for cause" removal); 46 U.S.C. § 301(b)(3) (FMC) (removal for "inefficiency, neglect of duty, malfeasance in office"). For further discussion on the grounds for removal, see infra "President's Recourse."

[27] See James M. Graham, Study on Federal Regulation: Vol. 1, The Regulatory Appointments Process, S. Doc. No. 95- 25, at 16 (1st sess. 1977) (noting that the creation of independent agencies dates back to 1887 when Congress established the Interstate Commerce Commission and observing that "[t]he commission form, as it has been created and developed by Congress over the past ninety years, is a determined attempt to isolate the agencies both from precipitous change and from control by the Executive Branch.").

[28] S. Doc. No. 95-25 (Vol. 1), supra note 27, at 16.

[29] Breger and Edles, supra note 24, at 1137.

[30] While most IRCs are multimember boards, Congress has listed some single headed agencies whose head serves a fixed term and have a for cause removal limitation as an IRC under 42 U.S.C. § 3502(5). See, e.g., Consumer Financial Protection Bureau, 12 U.S.C. § 5491(c).

[31] Mem. from OMB to Heads of Executive Departments and Establishments on Revision of Circular A-19, Revised, Dated July 31, 1972: Legislative Coordination and Clearance (Sept. 20, 1979), http://www.whitehouse.gov/omb/ circulars_a019/.

[32] See, e.g., Exec. Order No. 12866, § 6.

[33] 31 U.S.C. § 1108(b)(1); see also OMB Circular A-11 (Aug. 2012), http://www.whitehouse.gov/sites/default/files/ omb/assets/a11_current_year/a_11_2012.pdf.

[34] See, e.g., Mem. from Peter R. Orszag, Director of OMB, to the Heads of Departments and Agencies on Legislative Coordination and Clearance (Jan. 27, 2009), http://www.whitehouse.gov/sites/default/files/omb/assets/ memoranda_fy2009/m09-09.pdf; Exec. Order No. 12866, 58 Fed. Reg. 51735 (Oct. 4, 1993) (subjecting agency action to OMB review); OMB, Circular A-11 (Aug. 2012), http://www.whitehouse.gov/sites/ default/files/ omb/assets/ a11_current_year/a_11_2012.pdf.

[35] 12 U.S.C. § 250. The financial regulatory agencies include the SEC, Federal Reserve, FDIC, Comptroller of the Currency, the FHFA, and the National Credit Union Administration.

[36] 19 U.S.C. § 2232 ("... estimated expenditures and proposed appropriations [for the USITC] shall be transmitted to the President ... and shall be included by him in the Budget without revision, and the Commission shall not be considered to be department or establishment for purposes of such chapter."); see also 47 U.S.C. § 154(k).

[37] For instance, § 1 of EO 12866 sets forth a "Statement of Regulatory Philosophy and Principles," which requires agencies to critically examine their existing regulations, and § 4 commands each agency to submit an annual "Regulatory Plan" to OIRA.

[38] OIRA was established by the PRA, 44 U.S.C. §§ 3501-3520, to review agency information collection requests, but was not statutorily authorized to conduct centralized review of agency rulemaking as required under Exec. Order No. 12866.

[39] Some other portions of the Executive Order apply to IRCs. See, e.g., Exec. Order No. 12866 at § 4(b)-(c).
[40] Exec. Order. No. 12866 § 3(b). In turn, 44 U.S.C. § 3502(5) defines "independent regulatory agency" by establishing a non-exhaustive list of IRCs that are agencies "designated by statute as a Federal independent regulatory agency or commission." See supra note 23.
[41] Exec. Order No. 12866 at § 6(a)(3).
[42] Id. at § 3(f).
[43] Id. at § 6(a)(3)(A).
[44] Id.
[45] Id. at § 6(a)(3)(B).
[46] Id.
[47] Regulatory actions that fall within the first category of "significant regulatory action" are "economically significant" rules.
[48] OMB Circular A-4 provides agencies with guidance on how to conduct an adequate cost-benefit analysis and what specifically needs to be considered by the agency and submitted to OIRA. OMB Circular A-4, Regulatory Analysis (Sept. 17, 2003), http://www.whitehouse.gov/omb/circulars_a004_a-4.
[49] Exec. Order No. 12866 at § 6(a)(3)(C).
[50] Id. at § 6(b)(2). This review period may be extended once for an additional 30 days or indefinitely if requested by the head of the agency. Id.
[51] Id. at § 8. See Envtl. Def. Fund v. Thomas, 627 F. Supp. 566 (D.D.C. 1986) (holding that agency may publish final rule if waiting for OIRA review will cause issuing agency to miss a statutory deadline).
[52] Id. at § 6(b)(3).
[53] For analysis of how OIRA conducts this centralized review, see CRS Report RL32397, Federal Rulemaking: The Role of the Office of Information and Regulatory Affairs, coordinated by Maeve P. Carey.
[54] Exec. Order No. 12866, § 8.
[55] A thorough summary of the unitary executive theory can be found in Steven G. Calabresi and Kevin H. Rhodes, The Structural Constitution: Unitary Executive, Plural Judiciary, 105 Harv. L. Rev. 1153 (1992).
[56] U.S. Const., Art. II, §§ 1, 3.
[57] See, e.g., Saikrishna Prakash, Hail to the Chief Administrator: The Framers and the President's Administrative Powers, 102 Yale L.J. 991, 991 (1993) ("Historical evidence ... indicates that the Framers attempted to establish an executive who alone is accountable for executing federal law and who has the authority to control its administration.").
[58] Id. at 992.
[59] Proposed Executive Order Entitled "Federal Regulation, 5 Op. Off. Legal Counsel 59, 60 (1981) [hereinafter 1981 OLC Opinion].
[60] U.S. Const., Art. II, § 3.
[61] 1981 OLC Opinion, supra note 59 at 60-61.
[62] Myers v. United States, 272 U.S. 52, 135 (1926).
[63] The memorandum also notes that requesting information on the costs and benefits of proposed regulation is within his constitutional powers under the Opinions Clause of Article II. See 1981 OLC Opinion, supra note 59, at 62.
[64] Elena Kagan, Article: Presidential Administration, 114 Harv. L. Rev. 2245 (2001).
[65] Id. at 2327.
[66] Id. at 2327-28.

[67] Id. at 2327.

[68] See id.

[69] 343 U.S. 579 (1952) (holding President Truman's executive order directing the seizure of steel mills to be unconstitutional because Congress had not delegated the power to do so to the President and the action was essentially a legislative act) [hereinafter Youngstown]. Although Justice Black wrote the majority opinion, Justice Jackson's concurring opinion establishing a tripartite framework of presidential power has proven to be the most influential opinion of the Supreme Court decision.

[70] Id. at 635-38. (Jackson, J. concurring).

[71] Id. at 635, 637.

[72] Id. at 637.

[73] Id.

[74] Id. at 637-38. For example, his authority to act as Commander-in-Chief would be an exclusive Article II power. U.S. Const., Art. II, § 2, cl. 1.

[75] However, Kagan's argument that Congress has implicitly granted the President power over executive agency decisions could be viewed as an argument that would place the action in Justice Jackson's first category, thus giving the President maximum power to act in this area. See Kagan, supra note 64.

[76] Youngstown, 343 U.S. at 637.

[77] See, e.g., Jeffrey S. Lubbers, A Guide to Federal Agency Rulemaking 30 (4th ed. 2006) (noting the "fairly broad agreement that [OIRA review] is not only legal, but that if properly administered, it is essential to effective executive branch management").

[78] See 1981 OLC Opinion, supra note 59, at 60-61.

[79] Congress has not taken any legislative action against the President for implementing centralized review.

[80] Morton Rosenberg, Beyond the Limits of Executive Power: Presidential Control of Agency Rulemaking Under Executive Order 12,291, 80 Mich. L. Rev. 193 (1981).

[81] Legislative vetoes have since been determined unconstitutional by the Supreme Court in INS v. Chadha, 462 U.S. 919 (1983).

[82] Rosenberg, supra note 80, at 221-34.

[83] Abner S. Greene, Checks and Balances in an Era of Presidential Lawmaking, 61 U. Chi. L. Rev. 123, 128 (1994).

[84] See Rosenberg, supra note 80, at 197 ("The wording may thus suggest oversight of execution by others rather than direct execution by the President.").

[85] See id. at 233-34.

[86] See, e.g., Kagan, supra note 64, at 2384 (noting that centralized review "within broad but certain limits, both satisfies legal requirements and promotes the values of administrative accountability and effectiveness."); Administrative Conference of the United States, Recommendation 88-9, Presidential Review of Agency Rulemaking (1988), http://www.acus.gov/wp-content/uploads/2011/10/88-9.pdf; American Bar Association, Recommendation and Report 302 (1991), http://www.americanbar.org/content/dam/aba/directories/policy/1990_am_302.pdf.

[87] Jeffrey S. Lubbers, A Guide to Federal Agency Rulemaking 30 (4th ed. 2006).

[88] Although no courts have reached the constitutional questions raised by these executive orders, at least one court has acknowledged the constitutional issues raised by the OIRA review process. Pub. Citizen Health Res. Group v. Tyson, 796 F.2d 1479, 1507 (D.C. Cir. 1986) (reversing agency's decision based on the administrative record and avoiding the separation of powers issue presented, but noting that OIRA participation in rulemaking "presents

difficult constitutional questions concerning the executive's proper role in administrative proceedings"); see also New York v. Reilly, 969 F.2d 1147, 1152 (D.C. Cir. 1992) (holding that although the EPA "reevaluated its conclusions" regarding the issuance of a rule due to determinations from OMB that the rule failed to "meet the benefit/cost requirements... laid out in Executive Order 12291," the EPA still based its decisions on its own expertise and the refusal to issue the rule remained valid).

[89] Sierra Club v. Costle, 657 F.2d 298, 405-06 (D.C. Cir. 1981).

[90] Id. at 406.

[91] See, e.g., American Bar Association, Section of Administrative Law and Regulatory Practice, Letter to OIRA (Mar. 16, 2009), http://www.reginfo.gov/public/jsp/EO/fedRegReview/ABANET_comments.pdf.

[92] The first draft of President Carter's executive order, which imposed a number of procedural requirements on agency rulemaking, was ambiguous so that it might have applied to independent agencies. Exec. Order No. 12044, 43 Fed. Reg. 12,661 (1978) (entitled "Improving Government Regulations"). See also Harold H. Bruff, Presidential Power and Administrative Rulemaking, 88 Yale L.J. 451, 466 n.72 (1979).

[93] See Sally Katzen, Conference Summary: Can Greater Use of Economic Analysis Improve Regulatory Policy at Independent Regulatory Commissions?, at 2-3 (Apr. 2011), http://www.rff.org/Documents/Events/ Workshops%20and%20Conferences. See also Peter L. Strauss and Cass R. Sunstein, The Role of the President and OMB in Informal Rulemaking, 38 Admin. L. Rev. 181, 202 (1986) (In describing why IRCs were excepted from the executive order, the authors remarked: "This decision was based largely on fear of the congressional reaction to any such effort rather than on a judgment that the President lacked the necessary constitutional power." Id.).

[94] See Moreno, supra note 19, at 461, 494-96 (1994).

[95] 1981 OLC Opinion, supra note 59, at 60.

[96] Id. at 60. (citing Myers v. United States, 272 U.S. 52 (1926) (noting that while Congress can imbue cabinet officers with the power to appoint inferior officers and place incidental regulations and restrictions on when such department heads can exercise their power of removal, Congress may not involve itself directly in the removal process. Id. at 161.)).

[97] OLC observed: "It would be anomalous to attribute to Congress an intention to immunize from presidential supervision those who are, by force of Article II, subject to removal when their performance in exercising their statutory duties displeases the President." 1981 OLC Opinion, supra note 59, at 61.

[98] 295 U.S. 602 (1935) [hereinafter Humphrey's Executor].

[99] Id. The Court distinguished its holding in from Myers by stating that Myers was limited to "purely executive officers," as "such an officer [i.e., the postmaster] is merely one of the units in the executive department and, hence, inherently subject to the exclusive and illimitable power of removal by the Chief Executive, whose subordinate and aid he is." Id. at 627.

[100] Id. at 619-20.

[101] Id. at 628-29 (emphasis in the original). The Supreme Court ruled that the legislative and judicial functions envisioned by the statute necessarily placed the FTC outside the scope of complete presidential control. Id.

[102] Mem. for the Hon. David Stockman, Director of OMB, from Larry L. Simms, Acting Ass't Atty. Gen., Off. of Legal Counsel 7 (Feb. 12, 1981), reprinted in Role of OMB in Regulation: Hearing Before the Subcomm. on Oversight and Investigations of the H. Comm. on Energy and Commerce, 97th Cong., 1st Sess. 158 (1981) [hereinafter Second

1981 OLC Opinion]. OLC cautioned: "If the dicta of [the decision] are taken at face value, the President's constitutional power to supervise the independent agencies is limited to his power of appointment, and none of the proposed Executive Order's requirement may legally be applied to the independent agencies." Id. at 160.

103 Second 1981 OLC Opinion, supra note 102, at 160. Other scholars have also proposed treating insulation from presidential control or oversight differently for purposes of administrative adjudications compared to policy decisions, rulemakings and enforcement actions. See, e.g., Kavanaugh, supra note 25, at 1474.

104 Second 1981 OLC Opinion, supra note 102, at 160-61. Where the IRCs and executive agencies overlap in enforcement, the policies adopted by an IRC can affect those of executive agencies. See Harold H. Bruff, Presidential Management of Agency Rulemaking, 57 Geo. Wash. L. Rev. 533, 591 (1988-1989).

105 Second 1981 OLC Opinion, supra note 102, at 167-68.

106 Id. at 162. See also Mem. for Simon Lazarus, Assoc. Dir. Domestic Council, from John Harmon, Ass't Atty. Gen., Off. of Legal Counsel (Jul. 22, 1977) (concluding President Carter has authority to extend to IRCs an executive order designed to improve the administrative process within the executive branch) (citing James M. Landis, Report on Regulatory Agencies to the President Elect, reprinted in S. Doc. 91-49, Separation of Powers and Independent Agencies, at 1339 (1960) ("The congestion of the dockets of the agencies ... the failure to evolve policies ... are all part of the President's constitutional concern to see that the laws are faithfully executed. The outcome of any particular adjudicatory matter is, however, as much beyond his concern, except where he has a statutory responsibility to intervene ... ")).

107 See supra notes 55 to 58 and accompanying text.

108 Strauss and Sunstein, supra note 93, at 204.

109 Id. at 203.

110 Robert W. Hahn and Cass R. Sunstein, A New Executive Order for Improving Federal Regulation? Deeper and Wider Cost-Benefit Analysis, 150 U. Pa. L. Rev. 1489, 1534 (2002).

111 Id. at 1534.

112 Id.

113 Id. at 1536. To support their argument for a broad interpretation, Hahn and Sunstein observe that the Court in Bowsher v. Synar, 478 U.S. 714 (1986), held that the terms of removal applicable to a legislative branch officer were "very broad ... [and] could sustain removal ... for any number of actual or perceived transgressions of the legislative will." Id. at 729.

114 Hahn and Sunstein, supra note 110, at 1536.

115 487 U.S. 654 (1988) [hereinafter Morrison].

116 See Bruff, supra note 104, at 590-593.

117 Morrison, 487 U.S. at 691.

118 Bruff, supra note 104, at 591.

119 Id. at 592.

120 See supra notes 69 to 74 and accompanying text.

121 Youngstown, 343 U.S. at 637-38 (Jackson, J. concurring).

122 See Moreno, supra note 19, at 510 n.318.

123 Youngstown, 343 U.S. at 637.

124 Vesting Clause, U.S. Const., Art. II, § 1, cl. 1 ("The executive Power shall be vested in a President of the United States of America."); Take Care Clause, U.S. Const., Art. II, § 3 ("[H]e shall take Care that the Laws be faithfully executed.").

[125] See, e.g., S. 981, The Regulatory Improvement Act of 1997, 105th Cong., 1st sess. (1997).

[126] 1981 OLC Opinion, supra note 59, at 64 (stating the President has no authority to "reject an agency's ultimate judgment, delegated to it by law, that potential benefits outweigh the costs, that priorities under the statute compel a particular course of action, or that adequate information is available to justify regulation.").

[127] 1981 OLC Opinion, supra note 59, at 62. Other options for the President to take enforcement against the agency would be to modify its budget request amount or to request Congress to overturn the rule by legislation. However, the effectiveness of the President's reprimand against the agency would be dependent on congressional action.

[128] U.S. Const., Art. II § 2, cl. 2.

[129] Keim v. United States, 177 U.S. 290, 293-94 (1900) (citing Ex Parte Hennen, 38 U.S. (13 Pet.) 230, 259 (1839) ("In the absence of all constitutional provision or statutory regulation, it would seem to be a sound and necessary rule to consider the power of removal as incident to the power of appointment.")).

[130] See, e.g., 12 U.S.C. § 242 (Federal Reserve).

[131] See, e.g., 5 U.S.C. § 7104 (Federal Labor Relations Authority); 28 U.S.C. § 991 (U.S. Sentencing Commission).

[132] See PCAOB, 130 S. Ct. at 3215 (Breyer, J., dissenting) (Appendix D to Justice Breyer's dissent listed 29 departments and other agencies the heads of which are not subject to any statutory for cause removal protection and which have some of the traits which suggest independence).

[133] 357 U.S. 349 (1958) [hereinafter Wiener]. The Commission was composed of three persons appointed by the President with the advice and consent of the Senate. The Commission was to expire after a set number of years, and it is this time limit that acted as "the mode by which the tenure of the Commissioners was defined, and Congress made no provision for removal ... " Id. at 350.

[134] 62 Stat. 1240 (1948).

[135] Wiener, 357 U.S. at 354. ("The Commission was established as an adjudicating body with all the paraphernalia by which legal claims are put to the test of proof, with finality of determination 'not subject to review by any other official of the United States or by any court by mandamus or otherwise.'" Id.).

[136] "If ... the War Claims Act precluded the President from influencing the Commission in passing on a particular claim ... it must be inferred that Congress did not wish to have hang over the Commission the Damocles' sword of removal by the President for no reason other than that he preferred to have on that Commission men of his own choosing." Id. at 356.

[137] Wiener, 357 U.S. at 355 (citing Humphrey's Executor, 295 U.S. at 629).

[138] Id. at 356. As part of its conclusion, the Court also stated that "no such power of [at will] removal is given to the President directly by the Constitution." Id. While it has been long held that "the power of removal is incident to the power of appointment" absent a provision to the contrary, this statement from Wiener could be interpreted as indicating that, within the context of IRCs, there is some inherent constitutional limitation on the President's power to remove members at will.

[139] It is important to note that the Supreme Court decision in Morrison v. Olson, 487 U.S. 654 (1988), has modified the analysis on whether a restriction on removal is constitutional. After Morrison, the structure and characterization of an agency are no longer the controlling factors in determining who is removable at will, rather the "real question is whether the removal restrictions ... impede the President's ability to perform his constitutional duty." Id. at 691. The new test on removal is likely applicable where it is clear there exists a

restriction on removal, as was the case in Morrison. According to Breger and Edles, supra note 24, the "threshold question remains whether Congress intended to confer some form of statutory protection on government officials," in which case the Court's approach in Wiener may serve as a more appropriate guide in determining whether a for cause removal limitation may be inferred. See id. at 1144 n.163.

140 Swan v. Clinton, 100 F.3d 973, 981-83 (D.C. Cir. 1996).

141 Id. at 983. The D.C. Circuit first reached this conclusion to address the contention that Board members serving in a holdover capacity could not be removed unless there was cause.

142 SEC v. Blinder, 855 F.2d 677 (10th Cir. 1988) (accepting appellants' assertion in their brief, that it is commonly understood that the President may remove a commissioner only for "inefficiency, neglect of duty or malfeasance in office." Id. at 681.). See also SEC v. Bilzerian, 750 F. Supp. 14 (D.D.C. 1990) (also reviewing the creation, structure and purpose of the SEC and finding that "it is generally accepted that the President may remove a commissioner for inefficiency, neglect of duty, or malfeasance in office." Id. at 16.).

143 FEC v. NRA Political Victory Fund, 6 F.3d 821 (D.C. Cir. 1993).

144 Other agencies without a "for cause" removal provision, which are not listed IRCs but that share traits of independence, may not have a removal provision read into their statutes because they are not analogous to the FTC and WCC. Notably, OLC has opined that it would "resist any further application of the Wiener rationale ... except with respect to officers whose only functions are adjudicatory." The Constitutional Separation of Powers between President and Congress, 20 Op. Off. Legal Counsel 124, 170 (1996). For example, OLC opined that the President may remove at will the members of the Advisory Council on Historical Preservation, despite the Council being listed in statute as an "independent agency." OLC followed the approach in Wiener and examined the legislative history of the Council and its functions, which were primarily executive in nature and not akin to other quasi-legislative/judicial independent agencies. 6 Op. Off. Legal Counsel 180 (1982). See also President's Power to Remove Members of the Federal Council on the Aging, 5 Op. Off. Legal Counsel 337 (1981).

145 For example, the FCC, FDIC, and USITC are IRCs whose establishing statutes do not have a removal provision.

146 Some confirmed appointees to statutorily protected positions may choose to voluntarily resign or leave quietly under threat of removal. For example, S. John Byington was a confirmed member of the CPSC who served a term set to expire in October 1978. The CPSC statute provides the President with the authority to remove a member only for "neglect of duty or malfeasance" in office. 15 U.S.C. § 2053. During his term in office, Mr. Byington's conduct came under investigation by the DOJ. While articles indicate that he was under considerable political pressure, there does not seem to be any direct evidence that the White House pressured him to resign. Nonetheless, Mr. Byington resigned in June 1978, prior to the expiration of his term in office. See Bailey Morris, Byington Out But Agency's Ills Continue, Washington Star at A2 (Feb. 9, 1978).

147 Breger and Edles, supra note 24, at 1145. See, e.g., Morrison, 487 U.S. at 692 (stating "we need not decide in this case exactly what is encompassed within the term 'good cause' under the [Ethics in Government] Act").

148 Humphrey's Executor, 295 U.S. at 618-19 (1935). President Roosevelt's initial request for Mr. Humphrey's resignation was on the grounds "that the aims and purposes of the Administration with respect to the work of the Commission can be carried out most effectively with personnel of my own selection." Id.

[149] Id. at 626. The FTC Act provides that a Commissioner may only be removed for "inefficiency, neglect of duty, or malfeasance in office." 15 U.S.C. § 41.

[150] Independent Counsel Reauthorization Act of 1987, S. Rep. No. 100-123 at 12 (1987).

[151] S. Rep. No. 100-123 at 12 (stating that DOJ's interpretation of the statute "completely misconstrues Congressional intent.").

[152] Wiener, 357 U.S. at 356.

[153] Bowsher v. Synar, 478 U.S. 714, 729 (1986) (holding that Congress could not assign executive branch functions to the Comptroller General, a legislative branch officer). The statute provided the Comptroller General could be removed by Congress for "(i) permanent disability; (ii) inefficiency; (iii) neglect of duty; (iv) malfeasance; or (v) felony or conduct involving moral turpitude." 31 U.S.C. § 703.

[154] Breger and Edles, supra note 24, at 1145 (referring to the argument of Lawrence Lessig and Cass R. Sunstein in The President and the Administration, 94 Colum. L. Rev. 1, 110 (1994)).

[155] Peter L. Strauss, The Place of Agencies in Government: Separation of Powers and the Fourth Branch, 84 Colum. L. Rev. 573, 667 n.402 (1984). This proposition could be further supported by the argument, discussed supra, that extending the centralized review requirements to the IRCs by executive order is constitutional because a broad interpretation of the for cause removal terms could indicate that Congress granted the President supervisory powers over the policy decisions of agencies.

[156] S. 3468, § 3(c). The agency is to submit "(A) a determination that the rule complies with the requirements and an explanation of that determination; (B) if applicable, an explanation why the independent regulatory agency did not comply with one or more of the requirements, based on the statutory provision authorizing the rule; and (C) a clear statement of the issues on which the agency agrees or disagrees with the [OIRA] Administrator's assessment of the rule." Id.

[157] The Supreme Court has held that there is a "strong presumption that Congress intends judicial review of administrative action." Bowen v. Michigan Academy of Family Physicians, 476 U.S. 667, 670 (1986). Under the APA, judicial review is presumed to be available unless another statute precludes such review of where "agency action is committed to agency discretion by law." 5 U.S.C. § 702.

[158] BLAK Investments v. Commissioner of Internal Revenue, 133 T.C. 431, 447 (2009).

[159] Id.

[160] Id.

[161] State of Michigan v. Thomas, 805 F.2d 176 (6th Cir. 1986) ("Given this clear and unequivocal intent that agency compliance with Executive Order 12,291 not be subject to judicial review, we hold that the Order provides no basis for rejecting the EPA's final action.").

[162] The 1981 OLC Opinion also notes that even without the provision specifically precluding judicial review, courts would likely determine compliance with the order to be non-reviewable because the "Executive Order has not been promulgated pursuant to a specific grant of authority from Congress to the President and thus lacks the 'force and effect of law' concerning private parties." 1981 OLC Opinion, supra note 59, at 68 (citing Independent Meat Packers Ass'n v. Butz, 526 F.2d 228 (8th Cir. 1975) (holding that the executive order could not be judicially enforced because it had not been issued pursuant to delegation from Congress)).

[163] 5 U.S.C. § 706(2). NEPA claims are made on this basis. NEPA does not provide a private right of action so suits are brought against agencies under the APA arguing that the agency action is arbitrary or capricious for failure to consider the environmental impacts of the

federal action. See Robertson v. Methow Valley Citizens Council, 490 U.S. 332, 345- 46 (1989) ("[R]espondents brought this action under the Administrative Procedure Act to obtain judicial review of the Forest Service's decision. Their principal claim was that the Early Winters Study did not satisfy the requirements of NEPA.")

[164] When the Commission engages in rulemaking, the Commission "shall ... consider ... whether the action will promote efficiency, competition, and capital formation." 15 U.S.C. § 80a-2(c).

[165] 5 U.S.C. § 706(2)(A).

[166] Chamber of Commerce of the United States of America v. SEC, 412 F.3d 133 (D.C. Cir. 2005).

[167] Id. at 143.

[168] Id. at 144.

[169] Id. at 144–45.

[170] 647 F.3d 1144 (D.C. Cir. 2011).

[171] Id. at 1148.

[172] Id. at 1150–53.

[173] Id. at 1156. See also American Equity Investment Life Ins. Co. v. SEC, 613 F.3d 166 (D.C. Cir. 2010) (vacating SEC rule on fixed indexed annuities based on insufficient consideration of costs and benefits because SEC did not evaluate existing state regulatory schemes when determining that new federal programs would promote efficiency).

In: Independent Regulatory Commissions
Editor: Ruben Meijer
ISBN: 978-1-62808-103-9

Chapter 2

INDEPENDENT REGULATORY AGENCIES, COST-BENEFIT ANALYSIS, AND PRESIDENTIAL REVIEW OF REGULATIONS*

Maeve P. Carey and Michelle D. Christensen

SUMMARY

When issuing regulations that have the full force and effect of law, agencies are required to follow certain procedures. The Administrative Procedure Act (APA) of 1946 set up the basic framework for rulemaking: agencies are required to publish a notice of rulemaking in the *Federal Register*, take comments on the proposed rule, and publish a final rule in the *Federal Register*. Since the passage of the APA, additional procedures have been established in various statutes, executive orders, and guidance documents.

One potential change to the rulemaking process that has been discussed over the past three decades and proposed in legislation in the 112th Congress is the extension of the requirements of Executive Order (E.O.) 12866 to the independent regulatory agencies, also known as independent regulatory commissions (hereafter referred to as IRCs). E.O.

* This is an edited, reformatted and augmented version of a Congressional Research Service publication, CRS Report for Congress R42821, prepared for Members and Committees of Congress, from www.crs.gov, dated November 16, 2012.

12866 contains two major requirements: first, it requires that agencies complete cost-benefit analysis (CBA) of "economically significant" rules, considering the potential costs, benefits, and feasible alternatives to proposed and final rules. Second, the order requires centralized review of "significant" rules in the Office of Management and Budget's (OMB's) Office of Information and Regulatory Affairs (OIRA). Historically, the IRCs have been exempted from requirements for CBA and centralized review. Senator Rob Portman introduced a bill in the 112th Congress, S. 3468, that would authorize the President to extend to the IRCs, by executive order, E.O. 12866's requirements for CBA and OIRA review. If the requirements of E.O. 12866 were extended to the IRCs, there could be significant implications for those agencies.

Potential Extension of CBA Requirements. Proponents of extending the requirements argue that subjecting the IRCs to CBA requirements and OIRA review could improve the quality of regulations issued by those agencies. On the other hand, extending CBA requirements and OIRA review to the IRCs could grant OIRA (and by extension, the President) the potential authority to influence or delay rulemaking proceedings, and such a requirement could potentially decrease the independence of the IRCs. The IRCs with fewer regulatory responsibilities that issue relatively fewer "significant" rules each year may find the additional requirements of S. 3468 minimally burdensome, even if their current cost-benefit practices are not as rigorous as what would be required under E.O. 12866. Conversely, the IRCs with greater regulatory responsibilities or the IRCs with recently expanded regulatory responsibilities may find the additional CBA requirements more burdensome. It is also possible that some IRCs may not have the staff with the technical expertise necessary to conduct cost-benefit analysis that is more extensive than their current requirements.

Potential Extension of OIRA Review. The second major element of E.O. 12866 is OIRA review of "significant" regulations. During the review process, OIRA examines each regulation to ensure that the agency followed the principles and procedures outlined in E.O. 12866, including the applicable requirements for conducting CBA, and that the regulation is consistent with the policy preferences of the President. Numerous individuals, including former OIRA officials and several administrative law scholars, have spoken in support of potential OIRA review of regulations issued by IRCs. Much of this support for OIRA review relies on the underlying premise that increased presidential control, through OIRA review, of rulemaking could improve both the rulemaking process within agencies and the quality of the regulations themselves. On the other hand, some have expressed hesitation or opposition to the extension of OIRA review to the IRCs, suggesting that the independence of the IRCs could be compromised and that OIRA review of IRCs' rules could lead to delay.

INTRODUCTION

When Congress enacts a statute, it often delegates rulemaking authority to federal agencies to implement the statute. When issuing regulations, agencies are required to follow certain procedures. The first and arguably most significant requirements of the rulemaking process were established by the Administrative Procedure Act (APA) of 1946.[1] The APA set up the basic framework for rulemaking: agencies are required to publish a notice of rulemaking in the *Federal Register*, take comments on the proposed rule, and publish a final rule in the *Federal Register*.[2] Since the passage of the APA, additional procedures have been established in various statutes, executive orders, and guidance documents. Potential additional changes to the rulemaking process have been discussed and proposed, including many proposals in the 112th Congress.

This report discusses one potential change to the rulemaking process that has been discussed over the past three decades and proposed in legislation in the 112th Congress: extension of the requirements of Executive Order (E.O.) 12866 to the independent regulatory agencies, also known as independent regulatory commissions (hereafter referred to as IRCs).[3] E.O. 12866 contains two major requirements: First, it requires that agencies complete cost-benefit analysis (CBA) of "economically significant" rules, considering the potential costs, benefits, and feasible alternatives to proposed and final rules. Second, the order requires centralized review of "significant" rules in the Office of Management and Budget's (OMB's) Office of Information and Regulatory Affairs (OIRA). Historically, the IRCs have been exempted from requirements for CBA and centralized review. Senator Rob Portman introduced a bill in the 112th Congress, S. 3468, which would authorize the President to extend to the IRCs, through the issuance of an executive order, E.O. 12866's requirements for CBA and OIRA review.[4]

If the requirements of E.O. 12866 were extended to the IRCs, there could be significant implications for those agencies. Proponents of extending the requirements argue that subjecting the IRCs to CBA requirements and OIRA review could improve the quality of regulations issued by those agencies. On the other hand, extending CBA requirements and OIRA review to the IRCs could grant OIRA (and by extension, the President) the potential authority to influence or delay rulemaking proceedings, and such a requirement could potentially decrease the independence of the IRCs.

This report begins with a brief overview of E.O. 12866 and the IRCs. The report then provides a detailed discussion of the two major requirements of the order and analyzes the potential changes to the order that have been proposed in the 112th Congress.[5]

EXECUTIVE ORDER 12866 AND THE IRCS

President William Clinton issued E.O. 12866 in 1993. The executive order, which still remains in place today, replaced E.O. 12291, which was issued by President Ronald Reagan in 1981.[6] E.O. 12291 had similar requirements for agencies to conduct CBA and send their rules to OIRA for review, but its requirement for centralized review applied to *all* rules, not just "significant" rules.

The parts of E.O. 12866 that require agencies to complete CBA and to submit their rules to OIRA for review do not currently apply to statutorily designated "independent regulatory agencies," nor did they under President Reagan's order.[7] The details of these two requirements are discussed more below (see sections entitled "Cost-Benefit Analysis Requirements Under Executive Order 12866" and "OIRA Review of Regulations Under Executive Order 12866"). The exemption of IRCs from various requirements provides them with an element of independence from presidential control.[8]

E.O. 12866 uses the definition of an independent regulatory agency established in 1980 by the Paperwork Reduction Act (PRA; 44 U.S.C. §3502(5)).[9] The independent regulatory agencies listed are as follows:

> The Board of Governors of the Federal Reserve System, the Commodity Futures Trading Commission, the Consumer Product Safety Commission, the Federal Communications Commission, the Federal Deposit Insurance Corporation, the Federal Energy Regulatory Commission, the Federal Housing Finance Agency, the Federal Maritime Commission, the Federal Trade Commission, the Interstate Commerce Commission, the Mine Enforcement Safety and Health Review Commission, the National Labor Relations Board, the Nuclear Regulatory Commission, the Occupational Safety and Health Review Commission, the Postal Regulatory Commission, the Securities and Exchange Commission, the Bureau of Consumer Financial Protection, the Office of Financial Research, Office of the Comptroller of the Currency, and any other similar agency designated by statute as a Federal independent regulatory agency or commission.[10]

The current exemption for the IRCs from presidential review of agency rulemaking is one of the indicia of agency independence. Other elements of independence that provide various degrees of insulation from presidential intrusion into the budgetary, regulatory, and litigation processes are (1) "for cause" removal protections for the agency heads; (2) structural designs; (3) exemptions from OMB clearance requirements for legislative proposals, testimony, and comments; (4) authority to bypass OMB when submitting the agency's budget, or to submit the agency's budget to OMB and Congress concurrently; and (5) independent litigation authority.[11]

The remainder of this report discusses the two main requirements of E.O. 12866 in greater detail and analyzes the possible implications of extending those requirements to the IRCs.

COST-BENEFIT ANALYSIS REQUIREMENTS UNDER EXECUTIVE ORDER 12866

The primary cross-cutting requirement for agencies to consider costs and benefits when issuing rules is found in E.O. 12866, which requires agencies to assess costs and benefits for "significant" rules, both at the proposed rule and final rule stage.[12] "Significant" rules are defined in the executive order as follows:

> Any regulatory action that is likely to result in a rule that may (1) have an annual effect on the economy of $100 million or more or adversely affect in a material way the economy, a sector of the economy, productivity, competition, jobs, the environment, public health or safety, or State, local, or tribal governments or communities; (2) create a serious inconsistency or otherwise interfere with an action taken or planned by another agency; (3) materially alter the budgetary impact of entitlements, grants, user fees, or loan programs or the rights and obligations of recipients thereof; or (4) raise novel legal or policy issues arising out of legal mandates, the President's priorities, or the principles set forth in the Executive order.[13]

Rules falling into the first category of this definition are considered "economically significant" rules. When issuing "economically significant" rules, Section 6(a) of E.O. 12866 requires agencies to perform a much more detailed CBA, assessing the costs, benefits, and "reasonably feasible alternatives" to the planned rule.

Other provisions of E.O. 12866 also make reference to the consideration of costs and benefits during the rulemaking process for all rules, not just "significant" rules. Section 1(b)(5) requires an agency to "design its regulations in the most cost-effective manner to achieve the regulatory objective" and to "consider incentives for innovation, consistency, predictability, the costs of enforcement and compliance (to the government, regulated entities, and the public), flexibility, distributive impacts, and equity." Section 1(b)(6) requires agencies to "assess both the costs and the benefits of the intended regulation and, recognizing that some costs and benefits are difficult to quantify, propose or adopt a regulation only upon a reasoned determination that the benefits of the intended regulation justify its costs." Finally, Section 1(b)(11) requires agencies to "tailor [their] regulations to impose the least burden on society," while "obtaining the regulatory objectives, taking into account, among other things, and to the extent practicable, the costs of cumulative regulations."

OMB Circular A-4

In September 2003, OMB finalized Circular A-4 on "Regulatory Analysis," which refined and replaced an earlier OMB guidance document providing good-guidance practices to agencies for conducting their CBAs.[14] The circular states that it was "designed to assist analysts in the regulatory agencies by defining good regulatory analysis ... and standardizing the way benefits and costs of Federal regulatory actions are measured and reported." The document provides some specific information that agencies should generally include in their analyses, such as the statutory or judicial directives that authorize the action; the underlying problem or market failure prompting the regulation; consideration of a "reasonable number" of regulatory alternatives; and both a cost-benefit analysis and a cost-effectiveness analysis. Circular A-4 remains the current OMB guidance for agencies preparing CBAs.

Executive Orders 13563 and 13579

In January 2011, President Barack Obama issued E.O. 13563 to supplement and re-emphasize the general requirements of E.O. 12866.[15] E.O.

13563, like E.O. 12866, stressed the importance of cost-benefit considerations in the rulemaking process. Specifically, Section 1(b)(2) of E.O. 13563 encouraged agencies to "tailor [their] regulations to impose the least burden on society, consistent with obtaining regulatory objectives, taking into account, among other things, and to the extent practicable, the costs of cumulative regulations"; and to "select, in choosing among alternative regulatory approaches, those approaches that maximize net benefits (including potential economic, environmental, public health and safety, and other advantages; distributive impacts; and equity)." E.O. 13563 also instituted a retrospective review of regulations, under which agencies were required to "consider how best to promote retrospective analysis of rules that may be outmoded, ineffective, insufficient, or excessively burdensome, and to modify, streamline, expand, or repeal them in accordance with what has been learned."

E.O. 13563 used the same definition of "agency" as E.O. 12866, thereby excluding the IRCs. However, on July 14, 2011, President Obama issued E.O. 13579, entitled "Regulation and Independent Regulatory Agencies."[16] In that order, President Obama encouraged the IRCs to voluntarily comply with the provisions of E.O. 13563, including the retrospective reviews of regulations as well as other general considerations, including "economic growth, innovation, competitiveness, and job creation."

COST-BENEFIT ANALYSIS BY THE IRCS: CURRENT REQUIREMENTS AND PRACTICES

The IRCs are exempt from many of the analytical requirements and guidance documents that are applicable to executive agencies, including E.O. 12866, E.O. 13563, and OMB Circular A-4. However, the IRCs may be required to conduct CBA or other regulatory analyses under crosscutting statutes, such as the Regulatory Flexibility Act of 1980 (RFA), or under the underlying statutes that provide them with rulemaking authority. In addition, the IRCs may conduct CBA or similar analyses as part of their internal rulemaking process, even if they are not statutorily or otherwise required to do so.

The following section summarizes select statutory provisions that require the IRCs to analyze the potential effects of their rules. This section covers nine IRCs: the Securities and Exchange Commission (SEC), the Commodity Futures Trading Commission (CFTC), the Consumer Financial Protection

Bureau (CFPB), the Federal Deposit Insurance Corporation (FDIC), the Office of the Comptroller of the Currency (OCC), the Board of Governors of the Federal Reserve, the Nuclear Regulatory Commission (NRC), the National Labor Relations Board (NLRB), and the Consumer Product Safety Commission (CPSC).[17]

Cross-Cutting Analytical Requirements

The following statutes contain analytical requirements that apply to all agencies of the federal government, including the IRCs:

- the National Environmental Policy Act (NEPA) of 1969 requires federal agencies to provide a detailed environmental impact statement for all major federal actions that will significantly affect the quality of the human environment;[18]
- the RFA requires all federal agencies to assess the impact of their proposed regulations on "small entities" (e.g., small businesses, small governmental jurisdictions, and certain small not-for-profit organizations) and conduct a "regulatory flexibility analysis" at the time certain proposed and final rules are issued;[19] and
- the PRA requires all federal agencies to assess and minimize the paperwork burden for individuals, small businesses, and others resulting from the collection of information (from 10 or more nonfederal persons) by or for the federal government.[20]

Agency-Specific Analytical Requirements

Additionally, the IRCs may be subject to analytical requirements contained within the underlying statutes that provide them with rulemaking authority. This section provides select examples of statutory agency-specific requirements.[21]

Securities and Exchange Commission. The Securities Exchange Act of 1934 (15 U.S.C. §§ 78a *et seq.*), the National Securities Markets Improvement Act of 1996 (P.L. 104-290; 11 Stat. 3416), and the Investment Company Act of 1940 (15 U.S.C. §§ 80a-1 *et seq.*) each provide the SEC with authority to promulgate rules, and each has provisions requiring the SEC to consider whether a proposed regulatory action will "promote efficiency, competition, and capital formation."[22]

The Securities Exchange Act states that

> The Commission and the Secretary of the Treasury, in making rules and regulations pursuant to any provisions of this chapter, shall consider among other matters the impact any such rule or regulation would have on competition. The Commission and the Secretary of the Treasury shall not adopt any such rule or regulation which would impose a burden on competition not necessary or appropriate in furtherance of the purposes of this chapter. The Commission and the Secretary of the Treasury shall include in the statement of basis and purpose incorporated in any rule or regulation adopted under this chapter, the reasons for the Commission's or the Secretary's determination that any burden on competition imposed by such rule or regulation is necessary or appropriate in furtherance of the purposes of this chapter.[23]

The National Securities Markets Improvement Act of 1996 requires the SEC to consider whether an action "will promote efficiency, competition, and capital formation" whenever it is "engaged in rulemaking and is required to consider or determine whether an action is necessary or appropriate in the public interest."[24] Under the Investment Company Act of 1940, when engaging in rulemaking pursuant to the act, the SEC is required to consider (1) "whether an action is consistent with the public interest"; (2) "the protection of investors"; and (3) "whether the action will promote efficiency, competition, and capital formation."[25]

In 2011, in *Business Roundtable v. SEC*, the D.C. Circuit vacated an SEC rule that would have required public companies to disclose information to shareholders regarding shareholder-nominated candidates for board of director positions. The court noted that the SEC has an obligation to "determine as best it can the economic implications of the rule" and ultimately vacated the rule, finding the SEC's action arbitrary and capricious under the Administrative Procedure Act (5 U.S.C. §§ 551 *et seq.*).[26]

Commodity Futures Trading Commission. The Commodity Exchange Act (7 U.S.C. §§ 1 *et seq.*) provides the CFTC with rulemaking authority and requires the CFTC to consider costs and benefits before issuing certain regulations. Section 15(a) of the act states the following:

> Before promulgating a regulation under this chapter ... the Commission shall consider the costs and benefits of the action of the

> Commission. The costs and benefits of the proposed Commission action shall be evaluated in light of - (A) considerations of protection of market participants and the public; (B) considerations of the efficiency, competitiveness, and financial integrity of futures markets; (C) considerations of price discovery; (D) considerations of sound risk management practices; and (E) other public interest considerations.[27]

Title IV of the Dodd-Frank Wall Street Reform and Consumer Protection Act (P.L. 111-203, hereafter the Dodd-Frank Act) amended certain provisions of the Commodity Exchange Act and expanded the rulemaking responsibilities of the CFTC. According to the CFTC Office of the Inspector General, in light of its existing analytical requirements, the CFTC Office of General Counsel and Office of Chief Economist created a template for cost-benefit analysis processes that should be followed when proposing rules under the Dodd-Frank Act. The template requires the CFTC to consider, but not monetize or quantify, costs and benefits. The template also allows the CFTC to use discretion to determine that, notwithstanding its costs, a particular rule is necessary or appropriate to protect the public interest.[28]

Consumer Financial Protection Bureau. Title X of the Dodd-Frank Act created the CFPB and provided it with the authority to "administer, enforce, and otherwise implement the provisions of Federal consumer financial law."[29] The act also established certain standards of rulemaking that the CFPB must adhere to when issuing rules. Specifically, the Dodd-Frank Act states that

> the Bureau shall consider - (i) the potential benefits and costs to consumers and covered persons, including the potential reduction of access by consumers to consumer financial products or services resulting from such rule; and (ii) the impact of proposed rules on covered persons, as described in section 1026, and the impact on consumers in rural areas.

Therefore, it appears that the CFPB is required to consider potential costs and benefits before issuing certain rules, but it is unclear how much detail would be required in the analysis.

Federal Deposit Insurance Corporation. The FDIC has rulemaking authority under Section 209 of the Dodd-Frank Act. While some provisions of the Dodd-Frank Act require consideration of certain benefits and costs, it does not appear that the FDIC would be required to conduct such analyses under its rulemaking authority.[30]

The FDIC is also provided rulemaking authority by the Riegle Community Development and Regulatory Improvement Act (Riegle Community Act, P.L. 103-325; 108 Stat. 2160). The Riegle Community Act requires federal banking agencies, including the FDIC, to consider the burden and benefits their regulations will have on depository institutions. A report prepared by the FDIC Office of the Inspector General noted that Section 302 of the Riegle Community Act states,

> In determining the effective date and administrative compliance requirements for new regulations that impose additional reporting, disclosure, or other requirements on insured depository institutions, each Federal banking agency shall consider, consistent with the principles of safety and soundness and the public interest - (1) any administrative burdens that such regulations would place on depository institutions, including small depository institutions and customers of depository institutions; and (2) the benefits of such regulations.[31]

Therefore, it appears that the FDIC is required to consider the potential benefits and administrative burden prior to issuing certain rules. However, based on the language of this statutory provision, the level of detail that would be required in the analysis is not clear.

Office of the Comptroller of the Currency. Section 315 of the Dodd-Frank Act amended the PRA and designated the OCC as an IRC. Previously, the OCC had been part of the Department of the Treasury, and therefore was subject to E.O. 12866 and OMB Circular A-4. As a listed IRC, the OCC is no longer subject to those requirements. As a federal banking agency (as designated by 12 U.S.C. § 1813), however, the OCC is subject to the same analytical requirements of the Riegle Community Act as the FDIC.

Board of Governors of the Federal Reserve System. The Board of Governors of the Federal Reserve System (hereafter referred to as the Board) has rulemaking authority under multiple statutes, including the Federal Reserve Act (12 U.S.C. §§ 221 *et seq.*) and the Bank Holding Company Act of 1956 (12 U.S.C. §§ 1841 *et seq.*). According to the Office of Inspector General for the Board, statutes related to the Board's rulemaking authority "generally do not require economic analysis as part of the agency's rulemaking activities."[32] However, as a federal banking agency, the Board is subject to the same analytical requirements of the Riegle Community Act as the FDIC and the OCC.[33]

Nuclear Regulatory Commission. The NRC is provided rulemaking authority under the Atomic Energy Act of 1954 (42 U.S.C. §§ 2201 *et seq.*) as well as the Energy Reorganization Act of 1974 (42 U.S.C. § 5841). The Atomic Energy Act, as amended, provides the NRC with the authority to "establish by rule, regulation, or order, such standards and instructions to govern the possession and use of special nuclear material, source material, and byproduct material as the Commission may deem necessary or desirable to promote the common defense and security or to protect health or to minimize danger to life or property."[34] According to an NRC issue paper, "courts have interpreted the AEA to mean that costs must not be considered by the NRC when it determines that a given regulatory action is necessary for adequate protection."[35]

However, the act also provides the NRC with the authority to adopt regulations that go beyond "adequate" protection and the NRC's internal rulemaking procedures permit more extensive CBA of those rules.[36] For example, the NRC is subject to regulatory analysis requirements under the "backfit rule," which establishes procedures for the development of modifications to power reactors and/or selected nuclear materials facilities that are licensed by the NRC.[37] Under the backfit rule, the NRC must perform detailed cost-benefit analysis of all proposed modifications to nuclear facilities that go beyond "adequate" protection and provide a "substantial increase in the overall protection of public health and safety."[38]

It appears that the NRC must adopt the regulations it determines are necessary to adequately protect the public from the risks posed by the materials and facilities it is regulating, notwithstanding the cost. However, it seems that the NRC also conducts more extensive CBA of regulations that go beyond "adequate" protection; and according to the NRC's FY2011 Regulatory Plan, the NRC "routinely conducts comprehensive regulatory analyses that examine the costs and benefits of contemplated regulations" based on "internal procedures and programs to ensure that it imposes only necessary requirements on its licensees."[39]

National Labor Relations Board. Generally, NLRB rules are promulgated under the authority in Section 6 of the National Labor Relations Act (29 U.S.C. § 156), which does not mention a requirement to conduct cost-benefit analysis as part of the NLRB rulemaking process. A preliminary examination of NLRB rules submitted to GAO over the past year found that only one was considered a "major" rule.[40] For this rule, the NLRB estimated costs but not benefits.[41]

Consumer Product Safety Commission. The CPSC is provided rulemaking authority under at least nine statutes, including the Consumer Product Safety Act (CPSA), the Federal Hazardous Substances Act (FHSA), the Child Safety Protection Act (CSPA), and the Poison Prevention Packaging Act (PPPA).[42] These statutes contain varying degrees of requirements for CBA and other regulatory analyses. For example, the CPSA requires the CPSC to conduct a preliminary regulatory analysis prior to publication of a proposed rule, which must be published in the *Federal Register* with the proposed rule. The regulatory analysis must contain, in part,

> a preliminary description of the potential benefits and potential costs of the proposed rule, including any benefits or costs that cannot be quantified in monetary terms and.... a description of any reasonable alternatives to the proposed rule, together with a summary description of their potential costs and benefits.[43]

In contrast, the PPPA states that the CPSC should consider the "reasonableness" of packaging standards of specified household substances, but it specifically states the CPSC is *not* required to conduct cost benefit analysis. "Nothing in this Act shall be construed to require the Consumer Product Safety Commission, in establishing a standard under this section, to prepare a comparison of the costs that would be incurred in complying with such standard with the benefits of such standard."[44]

In sum, the IRCs may be required to conduct some form of CBA or other regulatory analyses of certain rules under cross-cutting statutes or the underlying statutes that provide them with rulemaking authority. In some cases, the analysis required may be less rigorous or less detailed than that which would be required under E.O. 12866 and Circular A-4. The IRCs may also conduct CBA or similar analyses as part of their internal rulemaking process, even if they are not statutorily or otherwise required to do so. Finally, the IRCs may be exempted or statutorily prohibited from conducting CBA as part of their rulemaking process.

Table 1 summarizes the cost-benefit analyses of "major" rules[45] that were conducted by selected IRCs in FY2010, FY2011, and FY2012. In some cases, the IRCs "monetized" or in other ways quantified costs, benefits, or both. According to an OMB report, however, the IRCs are more likely to discuss and consider costs and benefits without monetizing or quantifying them.[46]

Table 1. Cost-Benefit Analysis of "Major" Rules Issued by Selected IRCs: FY2010 to FY2012

Agency	"Major" Rules Issued	Monetized Costs and Benefits	Monetized Costs Only	Provided Some Information on Costs or Benefits
Securities and Exchange Commission	25	0	14	24
Commodity Futures Trading Commission	15	0	5	12
Consumer Financial Protection Bureau	1	0	0	1
Federal Deposit Insurance Corporation	2	0	1	1
Office of the Comptroller of the Currency[a]	3	0	2	2
Board of Governors of the Federal Reserve	12	0	2	2
Nuclear Regulatory Commission	3	0	3	3
National Labor Relations Board[b]	1	0	1	1
Consumer Product Safety Commission[c]	2	0	2	2
Total[d]	57	0	26	43

Source: Office of Management and Budget, 2011 and Draft 2012 Reports to Congress on the Benefits and Costs of Federal Regulations and Unfunded Mandates on State, Local, and Tribal Entities, Appendix C. The OMB reports contained information for FY2010 and FY2011. Additional information for FY2010, FY2011, and FY2012 was obtained from the U.S. Government Accountability Office Federal Rules Database, http://gao.gov/legal/ congressact/fedrule.html, and from the Federal Register. In select cases, the reports from OMB and GAO differed in their assessment of the CBA conducted by the IRCs. When necessary, the rule published in the Federal Register was consulted to resolve differences in the two reports.

Notes: Searches of the GAO Federal Rules database and the Federal Register were conducted on October 15, 2012.

[a]. OMB did not provide information on the OCC. However, according to the GAO Federal Rules Database, the OCC submitted three "major" rules to GAO. The first

rule was issued jointly with the FDIC and the FRS, and was published in the Federal Register on January 28, 2010, prior to the enactment of the Dodd-Frank Act (75 F.R. 4636). At that time, the OCC was subject to the CBA requirements of E.O. 12866. The second rule was published in the Federal Register on July 28, 2010, one week after the enactment of the Dodd-Frank Act (75 F.R. 44656). The third rule was issued jointly with the FDIC and the FRS, and was published in the Federal Register on August 30, 2012 (77 F.R. 53060). According to the GAO rule reports, the OCC did not conduct CBA for the first rule. For the last two rules, the OCC conducted CBA and monetized costs but not benefits.

[b] OMB did not provide information on the NLRB. However, according to the GAO Federal Rules Database, the NLRB submitted one "major" final rule to GAO on August 30, 2011 (76 F.R. 54006). The GAO report for this rule states that the NLRB described both costs and benefits, but only monetized cost.

[c] According to the GAO reports, the CPSC did not conduct cost-benefit analysis of its two "major" rules. According to the Federal Register, however, the CPSC did conduct regulatory flexibility analyses, including monetization of potential costs to small entities.

[d] A total of 57 individual "major" rules were issued in FY2010, FY2011, and FY2012. Some of these rules were issued jointly by two or more IRCs. Consequently, the sum of the each column may be greater than the totals that are listed in the table.

In FY2010, FY2011, and FY2012, a total of 57 "major" rules were promulgated by the nine IRCs included in this analysis. Of those, 43 "major" rules contained some information on benefits or costs, though only 26 included monetized estimates of costs. None of the "major" rules included monetized estimates of benefits.

- The SEC issued 25 "major" rules, more than any other IRC. The SEC provided information on costs and benefits for all but one rule. Fourteen of the 25 rules promulgated by the SEC monetized costs but not benefits.
- The CFTC promulgated 15 "major" rules. The CFTC monetized costs for five of their "major" rules, and provided some information on costs and benefits for 12 rules.
- The Board of Governors of the Federal Reserve promulgated 12 rules, two of which monetized costs.[47]
- The remaining IRCs each issued fewer than five "major" rules. The OCC and NRC each issued three "major" rules. The NRC monetized costs for each of its rules, while the OCC monetized costs for two rules.

- The CFPB and NLRB each issued one "major" rule. The NRLB rule monetized costs. The CFPB did not monetize costs, but did include some information on costs and benefits.

There are several possible reasons why the cost-benefit analysis currently conducted by IRCs may not be as rigorous as the full analytical requirements contained in E.O. 12866 and Circular A-4. First, the statutory provisions that require the IRCs to conduct cost-benefit analysis vary in scope, and the analysis they require may be less rigorous than that which would be required under E.O. 12866. As shown previously, some agency-specific statutes require cost-benefit analysis, including monetized or quantified estimates of costs and benefits whenever possible. Others require consideration of potential costs and benefits, but do not require quantified or monetized estimates. Others require little or no analysis at all.[48]

In addition, the internal rulemaking practices of each IRC vary in scope. Some may require or encourage staff to follow the cost-benefit procedures in Circular A-4. Other IRCs may integrate some, but not all, of OMB's guidance into their internal rulemaking procedures.

Generally, the nature of the rules being promulgated by the IRCs may make it difficult to conduct rigorous, quantitative, cost-benefit analysis. Some rules, for example, may involve costs and/or benefits that are more difficult for the agency to quantify or monetize. In such cases, E.O. 12866 and Circular A-4 instruct covered agencies to conduct cost-effectiveness analysis (CEA), which involves qualitative discussion of costs and benefits, as opposed to the more rigorous cost-benefit analysis, which typically requires monetized estimates of both costs and benefits.

Finally, the resources and capacity to conduct cost-benefit analysis may vary from agency to agency. For example, concerns have been raised over whether agencies have a sufficient number of staff who are qualified to perform extensive, quantitative cost-benefit analysis.[49] This, in turn, may be impacted by the number of rules promulgated by the agency each year; particularly those rules that are subject to cross-cutting or statutory analytical requirements. As shown in *Table 1*, the number of "major" rules promulgated each year varies from agency to agency. The SEC, which issued highest number of rules between FY2010 and FY2012, created the Division of Risk, Strategy, and Financial Innovation (Risk Fin) in 2009 to enhance its capability to conduct economic analysis as part of their rulemaking process. However, comparatively smaller agencies and agencies that promulgate fewer rules may not have a sufficient number of staff with the expertise to conduct extensive quantitative cost-benefit analysis.[50]

ANALYSIS OF POSSIBLE EXTENSION OF CBA REQUIREMENTS TO IRCS

The main argument in favor of extending E.O. 12866's CBA requirements to the IRCs is generally that such review would encourage agencies to produce higher-quality rules. Proponents have argued that through the executive orders establishing such review, Presidents have encouraged the executive branch agencies to consider more carefully the burdens associated with regulations; extending the requirements to the IRCs may bring those considerations to those agencies as well. A previously mentioned proposal in the 112th Congress, S. 3468, would authorize the President to extend CBA requirements through the issuance of an executive order.

Some advocates for extending the executive order's CBA requirements maintain that it may lead the agencies to produce higher quality rules. For example, former OIRA Administrator Sally Katzen has suggested that extending the requirements for CBAs to the IRCs and having OIRA review of those CBAs would provide incentives to agencies to produce high-quality analyses, since "nothing focuses the mind like knowing that someone will be reading" their analyses.[51] Susan Dudley, another former OIRA administrator, expressed disappointment in congressional testimony that President Obama has not extended the requirement for analytical requirements or OIRA review to the IRCs. Among the reasons she identified for this concern was that most financial regulations, including regulations issued by the new Consumer Financial Protection Bureau, will not be "constrained by the sound principles and procedures outlined by the President."[52] Indeed, many of the regulations that have been and will be issued pursuant to the Dodd-Frank Act will be issued by IRCs.[53]

It is not entirely clear how and whether extending E.O. 12866's CBA requirements to the IRCs would change their current practices, given that many of the IRCs already have statutory requirements for various forms of CBA, even if they are not subject to E.O. 12866. To the extent that the agencies are already fulfilling statutory requirements for CBA, extending the E.O.'s requirements may create duplicative requirements for some of those agencies. The following section of this report examines more closely the potential effects of extending CBA requirements to the IRCs.

Potential Effects of Extending CBA Requirements to IRCs

If enacted, S. 3468 would authorize the President to extend, through executive order, the requirements for CBA that are currently found in E.O. 12866.[54] The potential effects that this change may have on the CBAs conducted by each IRC would vary depending on (1) the agency's current analytical practices, (2) the agency's mandatory and discretionary rulemaking responsibilities, (3) the number of "significant" and "economically significant" rules the agency issues each year, and (4) the agency's analytical resources, such as the technical expertise of staff who are responsible for conducting their cost-benefit analysis.

The effects of S. 3468 may be minimal for IRCs that currently have cost-benefit analysis procedures similar to those of E.O. 12866 and Circular A-4. For example, a 2011 report by the Office of the Inspector General (OIG) of the SEC stated that "the Commission's current rulemaking procedures are closely aligned with the requirements of E.O. 12866, E.O. 13563, and OMB Circular A-4."[55] The OIG noted that the analysis conducted by the SEC did not always consider the costs and benefits of regulatory alternatives, but the SEC sought comments on the costs and benefits of alternatives to their proposed rules whenever possible.[56]

Similarly, the report by the OIG of the OCC noted that, prior to adoption of the Dodd-Frank Act, the OCC had been part of the Treasury Department and had been subject to E.O. 12866 as well as other OMB guidance. According to the OIG, "accordingly, the requirements for economic analysis defined in OCC's rulemaking guide generally mirror those of EO 12866 and OMB Circular A-4." [57] For IRCs with current analytical practices similar to those of E.O. 12866 and Circular A-4, the additional requirements that could be imposed under S. 3468 may already be met by the analyses they are currently conducting.

For agencies whose current procedures are less rigorous than those of E.O. 12866 and Circular A4, the effects of S. 3468 may depend on the other three factors listed above. [58] For example, an independent agency with fewer mandatory or discretionary rulemaking responsibilities that issues relatively fewer "significant" rules each year may find the additional requirements of S. 3468 minimally burdensome, even if their current cost-benefit practices are less rigorous. Those agencies may also find that their current staff and other analytical resources will remain adequate, even if they are subject to the executive order and OMB guidance.

Conversely, the additional cost-benefit requirements may be more burdensome for agencies with relatively greater regulatory responsibilities and for agencies with recently expanded regulatory responsibilities. These agencies may not have the staff with the technical expertise necessary to conduct cost-benefit analysis that is more extensive than their current requirements. For example, in light of the increased regulatory responsibilities some IRCs face pursuant to the Dodd-Frank Act, some have suggested that IRCs should consult OIRA when conducting cost-benefit analyses. In May 2012, Commissioner O'Malia announced that the CFTC had recently signed a Memorandum of Understanding with OIRA to obtain technical expertise when conducting regulatory analyses of rules it plans to issue pursuant to the Dodd-Frank Act.[59]

The potential effects of S. 3468 may also be mitigated for IRCs whose rulemaking activities would be exempt from some or all of the requirements of E.O. 12866. Under E.O. 12866, agencies are exempt from certain analytical requirements if (1) measures of costs and benefits are difficult to quantify or monetize,[60] (2) the rule is being promulgated under an emergency situation, or (3) the agency is under a statutory or judicially imposed deadline that makes full compliance with the executive order impossible. For example, the report from the OIG of the Board of Governors of the Federal Reserve noted that the executive orders provide agencies with exemptions to the cost-benefit analysis requirements in "emergency situations or when an agency is obligated by law to act more quickly than normal review procedures allow." The report did not specifically state whether, or how often, the Federal Reserve might qualify for such exemptions.[61]

The Debate Over Cost-Benefit Analysis

In addition to the debate over the appropriate role for the use of cost-benefit analysis in the IRCs, a broader debate over the value of CBA has also taken place over the past several decades.

On one hand, former OIRA Administrator Cass Sunstein, an administrative law professor, has been a strong advocate of CBA, and he has written many articles and books examining its rise and defending its use. In his book *The Cost-Benefit State: The Future of Regulatory Protection,* written prior to his tenure at OIRA, Sunstein examined the increase in use and requirements for CBA, arguing that the use of CBA can lead to a much stronger regulatory system and better regulations in general. Throughout the book, Sunstein made many arguments in favor of the use of CBA. For example, he suggested that CBA can be used not only to ensure that the benefits of regulation justify the costs and that "government action is worthwhile," but that it can serve as a check against interest group influence over regulations. Interest groups, according to Sunstein, are capable of "fending off desirable regulation or pressing for regulation when the argument on its behalf is fragile. Here CBA, taken as an input into decisions, can protect democratic processes by exposing an account of consequences to public view."[62]

Similarly, some economists and others have argued that CBA "can be a powerful tool in informing regulatory decisions. Regulation uses a sizable amount of resources, so it is relevant to ask whether the benefits of regulation are worth the costs" and that "centralized oversight can help with interagency coordination, setting priorities, and implementing most cost-effective regulation."[63]

On the other hand, some have argued that the use of CBA does not necessarily improve agencies' regulatory decisions. For example, one scholar testified before the House Judiciary Committee in 2011 that

> cost-benefit analysis is itself a flawed technique for distinguishing between useful and counterproductive regulations ... the existing regulatory process already allows those affected by regulations to identify flaws in agency regulatory proposals and affords both regulated entities and agencies opportunities to fix problems such as overly costly or unfair regulation.[64]

The witness stated further that while estimates of costs and benefits can be useful in regulatory decision making, such estimates are full of uncertainty and should not be the sole basis for determining regulatory outcomes. He suggested that agencies can use comment periods, as enforced by the courts under the Administrative Procedure Act, to obtain information and identify the best regulatory alternatives.

Additionally, CBA requirements may have the potential to slow down rulemaking, which may at times be contrary to the public interest. For example, the SEC has come under criticism recently because the pace of issuing rules appears to have slowed, particularly rules that are required pursuant to the Dodd-Frank Act.[65] One reason cited for the slow pace of rules is that the SEC was attempting to fulfill its statutory requirements for CBA, particularly after a court recently struck down one of the Dodd-Frank Act's rules for having an inadequate analysis in the *Business Roundtable* case mentioned earlier. A related hesitation about the use of CBA is that adding further requirements to a rulemaking process that is viewed by some as already too burdensome and time-consuming could put an unnecessary strain on agencies to meet statutory and/or judicial deadlines and other requirements.

Another concern that has been raised over the use of CBA is that it may be more difficult to estimate costs and benefits stemming from certain types of rules—particularly for those in which costs and/or benefits may be difficult to quantify or monetize. This criticism has often been voiced in response to proposals that would require banking agencies to measure costs and benefits, where the potential benefits involve things such as lowering financial risk or reducing fraud in securities markets. In addition, one recently issued report stated that costs tend to be easier to monetize than benefits, especially when dealing with market risk, which may cause costs to be overestimated in general.[66]

In the early 1990s, administrative law scholars began to write about the "ossification" of the rulemaking process.[67] The argument behind the "ossification" thesis states that agencies are subject to so many requirements in the rulemaking process that they generally take longer to issue rules and may require more resources to do so, resulting in uncertainty for the agency or agencies involved and for the regulated industry. One unintended consequence is that as the number of rulemaking requirements increases, agencies may have more incentive to seek out other vehicles for policy implementation, such as through the issuance of guidance documents and other less formalized means of executing policy changes. Proponents of the ossification thesis may argue that if Congress or the President institutes additional CBA requirements for the IRCs, those agencies may attempt to find other less participatory and transparent means for implementing policy. In other words, the ossification of rulemaking can incentivize agencies to preserve their resources by avoiding the rulemaking process and instead taking other administrative actions, such as the issuance of guidance documents and non-legislative rules.

On the other hand, President George W. Bush's OIRA Administrator John Graham testified before Congress that his experience and a review of the literature demonstrates that the ossification theory may be exaggerated, and that agencies continue to issue regulations in a timely manner, despite the numerous procedural and judicial requirements.[68] Some academic studies have also called into question the ossification thesis. One study, for example, found that there was little evidence that additional procedural requirements cause substantial delay in rulemaking.[69]

OIRA Review of Regulations under Executive Order 12866

The second major requirement of E.O. 12866, in addition to the requirement for agencies to conduct CBAs for "economically significant" rules, is centralized OIRA review of regulations. Under the order, agencies are required to submit proposed and final "significant" regulations to OIRA, at which time OIRA has up to 90 days to complete its review.[70]

During the review process, OIRA examines each regulation to ensure that the agency followed the principles and procedures outlined in E.O. 12866, including the applicable requirements for conducting CBA, and that the regulation is consistent with the policy preferences of the President. As former OIRA Administrator nominee James Blumstein discussed in an article on centralized regulatory review, E.O. 12866 made very clear that one of its main objectives was to make agency regulations consistent with presidential policy. According to Blumstein, this was illustrated by the frequent usage of the phrase "the President's priorities," which appears ten times in the order.[71]

E.O. 12866's requirements for OIRA review of "significant" regulations supplanted and somewhat scaled back the requirements of President Reagan's E.O. 12291, which required that agencies submit *all* proposed and final rules to OIRA for review. Since President Reagan issued E.O. 12291, scholars of the administrative process have expressed both support for and concern over OIRA's role, and by extension, the role of the President, in the rulemaking process. Some of this discussion, especially in recent years, has focused on the issue of whether rules by the IRCs should be subjected to OIRA review. S. 3468 would authorize the President to extend the requirements for OIRA review to the IRCs.

Analysis of Possible Extension of OIRA Review to IRCs

Many administrative law scholars and other observers of the rulemaking process have expressed support for OIRA review, and some have spoken directly in support of extending the requirement for review to the IRCs. Much of this support for OIRA review relies on the underlying premise that increased presidential control, through OIRA review, of rulemaking could improve the both rulemaking process within agencies and the quality of the regulations themselves.

Sally Katzen has suggested that centralized review of regulations "facilitat[es] political accountability (the President takes the credit and gets the blame for what his agencies decide)" and can "enhance regulatory efficacy (that is, decisions that take into account the multitude of disciplines and the multitude of perspectives that can and should be brought to bear in solving problems in our complex and interdependent society)."[72] Others have suggested that the White House is in a unique position to identify rules under development that may conflict with a rule or rules under development in another agency; centralized oversight may provide a mechanism for coordination between and among agencies.[73]

Some organizations have also expressed support for the extension of OIRA review to the IRCs. The Administrative Conference of the United States (ACUS) has supported presidential review of IRC rulemaking. In 1988, ACUS expressed its opinion that presidential review should apply generally to federal rulemaking: "As a matter of principle, presidential review of rulemaking should apply to independent regulatory agencies to the same extent it applies to the rulemaking of Executive Branch departments and other agencies."[74]

The American Bar Association (ABA) has also endorsed extending presidential review to the IRCs. In 1990, the ABA House of Delegates adopted a recommendation endorsing ACUS's guidelines President Reagan's executive orders establishing presidential review of agency rulemaking. The resolution declared that "presidential review should apply generally to all informal federal rulemaking, including that by independent regulatory agencies."[75] In 2009, the Section of Administrative Law and Regulatory Practice of the ABA provided comments to OIRA regarding presidential supervision of agency rulemaking and declared that the "White House should extend Executive oversight to independent agencies."[76] In October 2011, the ABA also submitted comments on H.R. 3010, the Regulatory Accountability Act of 2011 (RAA). Various provisions of the RAA would have extended OIRA oversight to IRC rulemaking. The ABA declared that it "strongly support[s] this feature of the bill" and noted that it has "long favored extension of the oversight orders to independent agency rulemaking."[77]

While many administrative law scholars and other students of the regulatory process support the extension of some OIRA review of regulations to the IRCs, other individuals and organizations have expressed hesitation or opposition. Many of the criticisms echo those that arose immediately following the establishment of centralized OIRA review under President Reagan in 1981. The main concerns of critics of Reagan's initial decision to establish centralized OIRA review of regulations were two-fold. First, some critics felt that OIRA review was a mechanism through which President Reagan would institute a deregulatory agenda. However, that concern has largely receded, in part because every President since Reagan has continued the practice of OIRA review. Second, critics charged that Reagan was asserting too much power, potentially violating the U.S. Constitution's separation of powers doctrine by asserting too much control over executive agencies' regulations. That objection has also largely receded since the 1980s.[78]

However, a similar concern has recently been raised over the possible extension of E.O. 12866's requirements to the IRCs, which have been considered at times to be quasi-legislative in function.[79] Because the IRCs generally possess elements of independence such as "for cause" removal protection for their commission members and agency heads, it has been widely interpreted that Congress intended to insulate the agencies from presidential control.

> Perhaps the most primary current concern about the possible extension of presidential review to the IRCs is that such a practice could compromise the independence of those agencies, and that it may give the President an inappropriate amount of power or influence over the rulemaking decisions of the IRCs. Because OIRA is part of OMB and is, by extension, an agent of the President, the concern is that subjecting regulations to OIRA review may politicize the rulemaking process. As explained by Katzen and others, "past presidents have been reluctant to extend OIRA's role to the IRCs out of deference to Congress."[80]

Sunstein has also written in strong support of presidential review of regulations. In one article, for example, Sunstein and administrative law scholar Peter Strauss argued that "time has not undermined the ABA's conclusion in *Roads to Reform* that greater presidential control over the regulatory process is desirable" and that there was a "growing professional consensus" on the matter.[81] Strauss and Sunstein identified three factors in support of OIRA review:

> First, the President is in a good position to centralize and coordinate the regulatory process.... Second, the President is electorally accountable.... Third, the President, by virtue of his accountability and capacity for centralization, is able to energize and direct regulatory policy in a way that would be impossible if that policy were to be set exclusively by administrative officials.[82]

Based upon those three premises, Strauss and Sunstein argued that OIRA review should be expanded to the IRCs:

> From the standpoint of sound regulatory policy, fashioned in a process of informal rulemaking, we believe that there is no meaningful difference between the "independent" agencies and those agencies to which the executive orders are currently applicable. The two categories of agencies engage in regulatory activities that are, from a functional standpoint, indistinguishable. Indeed, often those activities concern the same or similar subject areas; consider the overlapping work of the Department of Justice and the Federal Trade Commission in the area of antitrust. The same considerations that justify a coordinating presidential role with respect to "executive" agencies apply with full force to those characterized as "independent." For these reasons, we believe that Executive Orders 12291 and 12498 should be applied to the latter set of agencies.[83]

Were centralized OIRA review of regulations instituted, the question arises as to what the consequences of that review should be. Many scholars have offered suggestions as to how to extend the requirements and protect the independence of the agencies by limiting the ability of OIRA to stop an IRC from issuing a rule. For example, Katzen has said that presidential review should be extended to the IRCs, but it should be done cautiously:

> While the way the Executive Branch agencies and IRCs conduct rulemaking is for all practical purposes the same, the differences between the two types of agencies in terms of their structure and their relationship to the President suggests that the review process of the "enforcement" of any requirement for economic analysis should not—possibly, cannot—be the same without compromising the independence of the IRCs when they do not acquiesce in OIRA's assessment.[84]

In a 2002 article, two administrative law scholars suggested that while subjecting IRCs to OIRA review would be a beneficial change to the nation's regulatory system,

> None of this suggests that the President, or OIRA, should be permitted to displace the decisions of the independent regulatory agencies. But it does suggest that a supervisory rule, leaving the ultimate decision to those agencies, would be entirely acceptable. To those who are skeptical of this conclusion, it might make sense to create a special, weaker system of oversight for the independent agencies, limited to procedural matters (and hence allowing no room for return letters). But we think that it would be desirable to keep a single system in place for all agencies, retaining the idea that if an independent agency ultimately seeks to issue a regulation notwithstanding OIRA objection, it is entitled to do so.[85]

The establishment of limited OIRA oversight of agency CBAs, through means such as allowing non-binding feedback from OIRA that can only be advisory, may assuage some concerns, particularly if the authority is clearly delineated. This appears to be the approach taken by sponsors of S. 3468. If enacted, the bill would authorize the President to issue an executive order requiring IRCs to submit their rules to OIRA review. OIRA would have the opportunity to provide a non-binding statement assessing the agency's compliance with the relevant CBA requirements. The statement would be placed into the administrative record for the rule and could be reviewed by a court if the rule, once promulgated, were ever to be challenged. OIRA would not have the authority to stop an IRC from issuing a rule with which the President does not agree. Furthermore, the bill explicitly states that compliance or noncompliance with the executive order's requirements for CBA or OIRA review would not be subject to judicial review.

Another question that arises is whether it is appropriate for the President to assert a requirement for OIRA review, as the past several presidents have clearly been hesitant to do, or whether it would be more appropriate for Congress to institute centralized review. Katzen has suggested that while Presidents have been reluctant to extend OIRA's influence over the IRCs out of deference to Congress and over concerns about the independence of those agencies, congressional authorization of such an extension would "go a long way to ameliorate any concerns in that regard."[86] Through enacting a statutory requirement or authorization for OIRA review of rules and/or CBAs, Congress would be giving its explicit approval.[87] In a similar argument about the desirability for congressional authorization of the President to make such a change, one administrative law scholar said in testimony before Congress that

> Presidents have not brought the commissions fully into the tent of their executive orders, on my understanding, only because they fear that the political costs to their relationship with Congress would exceed the benefits of their doing so. In the Paperwork Reduction Act, Congress can be thought to have drawn that line. You can, and perhaps should, erase it.[88]

While the main criticism of the potential of subjecting IRCs to OIRA review is that the independence of the agencies could be compromised, other criticisms have been raised as well. A separate issue that has at times frustrated critics of OIRA review is that the OIRA review process may actually favor the interests of industry. Immediately after the issuance of E.O. 12291, critics expressed apprehension that OIRA review would serve as a "conduit" for private industry's interests.[89] Some studies and media reports have suggested that industry plays a significant role in the outcome of regulations.[90] The extension of that argument would suggest that OIRA could potentially serve as another access point for industry to influence rulemaking at the IRCs.

A final concern that has been raised over the idea of subjecting IRC rules to OIRA review is that OIRA may lack the technical expertise that is often considered to be a strength of regulatory agencies, and that increasing the number of regulations to come under OIRA's purview could put a strain on its resources.[91] Regulatory agencies have individuals who become subject matter experts in very narrow areas in which they regulate. Given the size and scope of OIRA's responsibilities, officials at OIRA tend to be issue generalists, not necessarily specialists.[92] On the other hand, OIRA may not have substantive expertise in a particular regulatory field, but its general understanding and focus on regulations makes employees at OIRA properly suited to distinguish between regulations that "may lead to unintended and undesirable consequences."[93]

ADDITIONAL ANALYSIS OF S. 3468

While S. 3468 would authorize the President to make the two changes discussed and analyzed above, there are additional points worth emphasizing.

The scope of the rules that could be covered by an executive order issued pursuant to S. 3468 is slightly different that the scope of what E.O. 12866 currently covers. The bill has a narrower definition for "significant" rules. The definition of "significant" in S. 3468 omits two categories that are included in the definition of "significant" in E.O. 12866. Those categories are rules that "materially alter the budgetary impact of entitlements, grants, user fees, or loan programs or the rights and obligations of recipients thereof;" or rules that "raise novel legal or policy issues arising out of legal mandates, the President's priorities, or the principles set forth in the Executive order." In other words, rules that fall into those categories that are issued by IRCs would not be authorized by S. 3468 to be subject to OIRA review.

However, the definition of "rule" in S. 3468 is broader than the definition of "rule" in E.O. 12866, and could possibly include some guidance documents. S. 3468 references the definition of a rule as defined in section 551 of title 5 (the Administrative Procedure Act), rather than the definition used in 553, which is the section that defines "rule" for the purposes of notice and comment requirements.

Furthermore, as mentioned above, the bill clearly states that the compliance or noncompliance of an IRC with the requirements of an executive order issued pursuant to the bill could not be subject to judicial review. The potential consequences of what could occur if an IRC and OIRA disagree on the analysis or substance of a particular rule also are unclear.[94]

End Notes

[1] 5 U.S.C. § 551 et seq. For more information about rulemaking generally, see CRS Report RL32240, The Federal Rulemaking Process: An Overview, coordinated by Maeve P. Carey.

[2] The APA specifically authorizes federal agencies to dispense with its requirements for notice and comment if the agency for good cause finds that the use of traditional procedures would be "impracticable, unnecessary, or contrary to the public interest" (5 U.S.C. § 553(b)(B)).

[3] Executive Order 12866, "Regulatory Planning and Review," 58 Federal Register 51735, October 4, 1993.

[4] S. 3468 (112th Congress), introduced by Senator Rob Portman on August 1, 2012.

[5] This report does not provide any legal analysis of the possible extension of cost-benefit analysis or OIRA review of regulations to the IRCs. For an overview of the legal issues involved, see CRS Report R42720, Presidential Review of Independent Regulatory Commission Rulemaking: Legal Issues, by Vivian S. Chu and Daniel T. Shedd.

[6] For more information about these orders, see CRS Report RL32397, Federal Rulemaking: The Role of the Office of Information and Regulatory Affairs, coordinated by Maeve P. Carey.

[7] Certain parts of E.O. 12866 do apply to IRCs—such as the requirements that each agency (1) "prepare an agenda of all regulations under development or review" and (2) "prepare a

Regulatory Plan ... of the most important significant regulatory actions that the agency reasonably expects to issue in proposed or final form in that fiscal year or thereafter" (§4(b), the Unified Regulatory Agenda; §4(c), the Regulatory Plan).

[8] Commenters at an April 2011 Resources for the Future conference stated that both President Reagan and President Clinton obtained legal opinions from the Office of Legal Counsel at the Department of Justice stating that Executive Orders 12291 and 12866 could cover IRCs. However, the decision not to cover them was reportedly a political, not a legal, determination. See Sally Katzen, "Can Greater Use of Economic Analysis Improve Regulatory Policy at Independent Regulatory Commissions?" Opening Remarks, Washington, D.C., April 7, 2011, http://www.rff.org/ Documents/Events/Workshops%20and%20Conferences/110407_Regulation_KatzenRemarks.pdf, pp. 2-3.

[9] This list has been amended since 1980, most recently by the Dodd-Frank Wall Street Reform and Consumer Protection Act (P.L. 111-203, hereafter the Dodd-Frank Act). The agencies listed in this section of the U.S. Code have special procedures for OMB review of their information collection requests under the PRA. For more information, see CRS Report R40636, Paperwork Reduction Act (PRA): OMB and Agency Responsibilities and Burden Estimates, by Curtis W. Copeland and Vanessa K. Burrows.

[10] The United States International Trade Commission is one of the "other similar agenc[ies] designated by statute as a Federal independent regulatory agency" although it is not specifically listed in that provision of the U.S. Code. See 19 U.S.C. § 1330(f) (stating that the United States International Trade Commission "shall be considered to be an independent regulatory agency for purposes of chapter 35 of title 44, United States Code").

[11] For an in-depth discussion of characteristics of IRCs, see CRS Report R42720, Presidential Review of Independent Regulatory Commission Rulemaking: Legal Issues, by Vivian S. Chu and Daniel T. Shedd, pp. 3-5; Marshall J. Breger and Gary J. Edles, "Established by Practice: The Theory and Operation of Independent Federal Agencies," Administrative Law Review, vol. 52, no. 4 (Fall 2000), pp. 1144-1145; and Duke Law Journal's "Symposium: The Independence of Independent Agencies," vol. 137, no. 2&3 (April/June), pp. 215-299.

[12] For more information about other cost-benefit analysis requirements, see CRS Report R41974, Cost-Benefit and Other Analysis Requirements in the Rulemaking Process, by Maeve P. Carey.

[13] The definition of "significant" rules in S. 3468 differs slightly from the definition in E.O. 12866. See section below entitled "Additional Analysis of S. 3468."

[14] OMB Circular A-4, "Regulatory Analysis," September 17, 2003, http://www.whitehouse.gov/ omb/assets/ regulatory_matters_pdf/a-4.pdf. The circular took effect for "economically significant" proposed rules on January 1, 2004, and for "economically significant" final rules on January 1, 2005.

[15] Executive Order 13563, "Improving Regulations and Regulatory Review," 76 Federal Register 3821, January 21, 2011.

[16] Executive Order 13579, "Regulation and Independent Regulatory Agencies," 76 Federal Register 41587, July 14, 2011.

[17] Together, these nine IRCs issued 57 major rules (e.g., rules having a $100 million impact on the economy) in FY2010, FY2011, and FY2012. The Federal Trade Commission issued one major rule jointly with the Board of Governors of the Federal Reserve. The remaining nine IRCs listed in the PRA did not issue any major rules during that period.

[18] 42 U.S.C. §§ 4321-4347. The "trigger" for the analytical requirements contained in the NEPA has been challenged and defined in court. For additional information, see CRS Report R41974, Cost-Benefit and Other Analysis Requirements in the Rulemaking Process, by

Maeve P. Carey, and CRS Report RS20621, Overview of National Environmental Policy Act (NEPA) Requirements, by Kristina Alexander.

[19] 5 U.S.C. §§ 601-612.

[20] 44 U.S.C. §§ 3501-3520.

[21] Statutes that provide the IRCs with rulemaking authority were identified by reviewing a sample of the rules issued by each IRC and by reviewing information on regulations and rulemaking procedures contained on each IRCs website. Statutory provisions that require the IRCs to analyze the potential effects of their rules were identified by searching those statutes for variants of the terms "rulemaking," "regulation," and variants of the phrases "cost-benefit analysis" and "consider costs and/or benefits." In some cases where the IRC is provided with rulemaking authority under multiple statutes, a sample of statutes identified was examined.

[22] See, for example, 15 U.S.C. § 77b(b).

[23] 15 U.S.C. § 78w(a)(2).

[24] 15 U.S.C. § 77b(b).

[25] 15 U.S.C. § 80a-2(c).

[26] Business Roundtable v. SEC, 647 F.3rd 1144 (D.C. Cir. 2011).

[27] 7 U.S.C. § 19(a). Subsection (a)(3) states that these requirements do not apply to "(A) An order that initiates, is part of, or is the result of an adjudicatory or investigative process of the Commission, (B) an emergency action, or (C) a finding of fact regarding compliance with a requirement of the Commission."

[28] Office of the Inspector General, U.S. Commodity Futures Trading Commission, "A Review of Cost-Benefit Analyses Performed by the Commodity Futures Trading Commission in Connection with Rulemakings Undertaken Pursuant to the Dodd-Frank Act," June 13, 2011, http://www.cftc.gov/ucm/groups/public/@aboutcftc/documents/file/ oig_investigation_061311.pdf.

[29] 12 U.S.C. § 5512(a).

[30] See, e.g., 12 U.S.C. § 5551(c)(2) and 12 U.S.C. § 5512(b)(2)(A).

[31] Office of the Inspector General, Federal Deposit Insurance Corporation, "Evaluation of the FDIC's Economic Analysis of Three Rulemakings to Implement Provisions of the Dodd-Frank Act," June 13, 2011, p. 12, http://www.fdicig.gov/reports11/11-003EV.pdf.

[32] Office of the Inspector General, Board of Governors of the Federal Reserve System, "Response to a Congressional Request Regarding the Economic Analysis Associated with Specified Rulemakings," June 13, 2011, p. 6, http://www.federalreserve.gov/oig/files/ Congressional_Response_web.pdf.

[33] The Board also has rulemaking authority under two provisions of the Electronic Funds Transfer Act (EFT Act, 15 U.S.C. § 1693b), which was amended by the Dodd-Frank Wall Street Reform and Consumer Protection Act (P.L. 111- 203; 124 Stat. 1376, hereafter the Dodd-Frank Act).

[34] 42 U.S.C. § 2201(b).

[35] R.W. Borchardt, Executive Director for Operations, Nuclear Regulatory Commission, "Consideration of Economic Consequences within the U.S. Nuclear Regulatory Commission's Regulatory Framework," August 14, 2012, enclosure 3, p.1, http://www.nrc.gov/reading-rm/doc-collections/commission/secys/2012/2012-0110scy.pdf.

[36] 42 U.S.C. § 2232(a).

[37] 10 C.F.R. § 50.109.

[38] R.W. Borchardt, Executive Director for Operations, Nuclear Regulatory Commission, "Consideration of Economic Consequences within the U.S. Nuclear Regulatory

Commission's Regulatory Framework," August 14, 2012, p.4, http://www.nrc.gov/reading-rm/doc-collections/commission/secys/2012/2012-0110scy.pdf.

[39] U.S. Nuclear Regulatory Commission, Fiscal Year 2011 Regulatory Plan Statement of Regulatory Priorities, January 20, 2012, http://www.reginfo.gov/public/jsp/ eAgenda/Static Content/201110/Statement_3150.html.

[40] See National Labor Relations Board, "Notification of Employee Rights Under the National Labor Relations Act," 76 Federal Register 54006, August 30, 2011.

[41] U.S. Government Accountability Office, National Labor Relations Board: Notification of Employee Rights Under the National Labor Relations Act, GAO-11-951R, September 20, 2011, http://gao.gov/products/GAO-11-951R.

[42] See Consumer Product Safety Act, as amended (P.L. 92-573; 15 U.S.C. §§ 2051-2089); Federal Hazardous Substances Act, as amended (P.L. 86-613; 15 U.S.C. §§ 1261-1278); Child Safety Protection Act (P.L. 103-267); and the Poison Prevention Packaging Act (P.L. 91-601; 15 U.S.C. § 1471 et seq.). The CPSC maintains a list of the statutes that provide them with regulatory authority. The list may be found at http://www.cpsc.gov/businfo/ actreg.html.

[43] 15 U.S.C. § 2058(c).

[44] 15 U.S.C. § 1472(e).

[45] The definition of "major" rule is slightly different than that of "economically significant" rule. Under the Congressional Review Act, a rule is "major" if it is likely to result in "(A) an annual effect on the economy of $100 million or more; (B) a major increase in costs or prices for consumers, individual industries, federal, state, or local government agencies, or geographic regions; or (C) significant adverse effects on competition, employment, investment, productivity, innovation, or on the ability of United States-based enterprises to compete with foreign-based enterprises in domestic and export markets" (5 U.S.C. § 804(2)). In contrast, the definition of "economically significant" is found in E.O. 12866. OIRA maintains information on the number of reviews conducted each year of "significant" and "economically significant" rules, but does not keep data on the number of those types of rules issued each year. The information in Table 1 was obtained largely from the GAO Federal Rules Database, which contains reports on all "major" rules issued annually by agencies, including the IRCs.

[46] See Office of Management and Budget, Office of Information and Regulatory Affairs, 2011 Report to Congress on the Benefits and Costs of Federal Regulations and Unfunded Mandates on State, Local, and Tribal Entities and Draft 2012 Report to Congress on the Benefits and Costs of Federal Regulations and Unfunded Mandates on State, Local, and Tribal Entities, http://www.whitehouse.gov/omb/inforeg_regpol_reports_congress.

[47] While the Federal Reserve appears rarely to conduct cost-benefit analysis as part of its rulemaking process, it is important to note that many of its rules involved monetary policy, which may be exempt from analytical requirements under S. 3468, which is discussed more in detail later in this report.

[48] It is important to note that while the statutory requirements applicable to the IRCs may be less rigorous, they frequently apply to all of the rules proposed or issued, whereas the most rigorous analytical requirements of E.O. 12866 and Circular A-4 apply only to "economically significant" rules. For example, the internal regulatory analysis guidance issued by the NRC notes, "the NRC requires regulatory analyses for a broader range of regulatory actions than for significant rulemakings as defined in E.O. 12866" and, with certain exceptions, NRC's analytical requirements apply to "rules, bulletins, generic letters, regulatory guides, orders, standard review plans, branch technical positions, and standard

technical specifications." Nuclear Regulatory Commission, Regulatory Analysis Guidelines of the U.S. Nuclear Regulatory Commission, NUREG/BR-0058 Revision 4, September, 2004, p. 10, http://www.nrc.gov/readingrm/doc-collections/nuregs/brochures/br0058/br0058r4.pdf.

[49] For example, the OIG for the CFTC noted that cost-benefit analysis was controlled by CFTC's legal staff rather than economists, and that "consideration of costs and benefits was being approached as a legal issue rather than an economic one." Office of the Inspector General, U.S. Commodity Futures Trading Commission, "A Review of Cost-Benefit Analyses Performed by the Commodity Futures Trading Commission in Connection with Rulemakings Undertaken Pursuant to the Dodd-Frank Act," June 13, 2011, http://www.cftc.gov/ucm/groups/public/@aboutcftc/documents/file/oig_investigation_061311.pdf.

[50] Having sufficient staff with the expertise to conduct extensive quantitative cost-benefit analysis may also be an issue for agencies currently subject to E.O. 12866 and Circular A-4.

[51] Testimony of Sally Katzen, U.S. Congress, House Committee on the Judiciary, Subcommittee on Courts, Commercial and Administrative Law, Cost Justifying Regulations: Protecting Jobs and the Economy by Presidential and Judicial Review of Costs and Benefits, 112th Cong., 1st sess., May 4, 2011, p. 7, http://judiciary.house.gov/hearings/ pdf/Katzen 05042011.pdf.

[52] Testimony of Susan E. Dudley, U.S. Congress, House Committee on the Judiciary, Subcommittee on Courts, Commercial and Administrative Law, The APA at 65- Is Reform Needed to Create Jobs, Promote Economic Growth and Reduce Costs?, 112th Cong., 1st sess., February 8, 2011, p. 17, http://judiciary.house.gov/hearings/pdf/ Dudley0228 2011.pdf.

[53] For further information about the agencies responsible for implementing the Dodd-Frank Act, see CRS Report R41472, Rulemaking Requirements and Authorities in the Dodd-Frank Wall Street Reform and Consumer Protection Act, by Curtis W. Copeland. In a November 2011 report, GAO observed that regulations issued pursuant to the Dodd-Frank Act could be improved if agencies performed more rigorous analyses that fully incorporated the guidance in OMB's Circular A-4, despite the fact that they are not required to do so. U.S. Government Accountability Office, Dodd-Frank Act Regulations: Implementation Could Benefit from Additional Analyses and Coordination, GAO-12- 151, November 2011, http://www.gao.gov/assets/590/586210.pdf.

[54] As discussed later in this report, Presidents have been reluctant to extend CBA requirements and OIRA review to the IRCs, largely for political reasons and out of deference to Congress. Administrative law scholars have suggested that if Congress were to authorize such an extension, concerns about its appropriateness would be ameliorated (see section entitled "Analysis of Possible Extension of OIRA Review to IRCs"). An alternative approach would be for Congress to enact a statute requiring IRCs to comply with the E.O.'s requirements for cost-benefit analysis, or even creating a requirement in statute without tying the requirement for the executive order, rather than authorizing the President to extend the current requirements through an executive order.

[55] Office of the Inspector General, U.S. Securities and Exchange Commission, "Report of Review of Economic Analyses Performed by the Securities and Exchange Commission in Connection with Dodd-Frank Rulemakings," June 13, 2011, http://www.sec-oig.gov/Reports/AuditsInspections/2011/Report_6_13_11.pdf. The report from the OIG of the SEC, along with reports from the OIGs of the CFTC, FDIC, OCC, and Federal Reserve, were completed in response to a request from the 10 Republican Senators on the Senate

Committee on Banking, Housing, and Urban Affairs. On May 4, 2011, the Senators jointly requested that the OIGs provide them with information about the analytical requirements applicable to rulemaking in those five agencies. Each agency was asked to describe "any additional steps that the agency would have to take if it were subject to Executive Orders 13563 and 12866 and associated Office of Management and Budget guidance [Circular A-4]." See http://crapo.senate.gov/documents/RepublicanBankingCommitteeDoddFrankLetter.pdf for a copy of this letter.

56 Ibid. In addition, the SEC-OIG noted that the analysis conducted by the SEC is not always quantitative, and recommended that a larger portion of cost-benefit analysis should be conducted by the SEC's Division of Risk, Strategy, and Financial Innovation (RiskFin, or RSFI), who have the skills in econometrics and other expertise needed to perform quantitative cost-benefit analysis.

57 Office of the Inspector General, Department of the Treasury, "Dodd-Frank Act: Congressional Request for Information Regarding Economic Analysis by OCC," June 13, 2011, http://www.treasury.gov/about/organizationalstructure/ig/Documents/OIG-CA-11-006.pdf.

58 For example, the OIG reports for the CFTC and the FDIC both note that the agencies have internal guidance that encourage, but do not require, analytical practices similar in spirit to those in E.O. 12866 and Circular A-4. See Inspector General, U.S. Commodity Futures Trading Commission, "A Review of Cost-Benefit Analyses Performed by the Commodity Futures Trading Commission in Connection with Rulemakings Undertaken Pursuant to the Dodd-Frank Act," June 13, 2011, http://www.cftc.gov/ucm/groups/public/ @aboutcftc/documents/file/oig_investigation_061311.pdf and Office of the Inspector General, Federal Deposit Insurance Corporation, "Evaluation of the FDIC's Economic Analysis of Three Rulemakings to Implement Provisions of the Dodd-Frank Act," Report No. EVAL-11-003, June 2011, p. 1 of the Executive Summary, http://www.fdicoig.gov/reports11%5C11-003EV.pdf.

59 See Scott D. O'Malia, CFTC Commissioner, "Smart Regulatory Reform and the Perils of High-Frequency Regulation," remarks at Outlook for ITC Markets event, May 31, 2012, http://www.cftc.gov/PressRoom/ SpeechesTestimony/opaomalia-14.

60 IRCs have cited their inability to quantify costs or benefits as a reason for not conducting full cost-benefit analysis. For example, see the GAO Major Rule Reports for two rules issued by the CFTC, "Core Principles and Other Requirements for Designated Contract Markets" and "Customer Clearing Documentation, Timing of Acceptance for Clearing, and Clearing Member Risk Management" at http://gao.gov/assets/600/592157.pdf and http://gao.gov/assets/ 600/590519.pdf, respectively. It is unclear under what circumstances IRCs may be exempt from CBA due to the difficulty of quantifying costs and/or benefits.

61 Office of the Inspector General, Board of Governors of the Federal Reserve System, "Response to a Congressional Request Regarding the Economic Analysis Associated with Specified Rulemakings," June 13, 2011, p. 6, http://www.federalreserve.gov/oig/files/Congressional_Response_web.pdf. It is also important to note that under Sec. 2 of S. 3468, as introduced, expanded cost-benefit analysis would not apply to "a rule of the Board of Governors of the Federal Reserve System or the Federal Open Market Committee relating to monetary policy."

62 Cass R. Sunstein, The Cost-Benefit State: The Future of Regulatory Protection (Chicago: American Bar Association, 2002), pp. 6-10. On the other hand, some have argued that OIRA, which currently reviews most agencies' CBAs, may act as a conduit for industry interests; this concern is discussed later in the report in the section on OIRA review.

[63] Robert W. Hahn and Paul C. Tetlock, "Has Economic Analysis Improved Regulatory Decisions?" Journal of Economic Perspectives, vol. 22, no. 1 (Winter 2008), p. 68.

[64] Testimony of Robert L. Glicksman, U.S. Congress, House Committee on the Judiciary, Subcommittee on Courts, Commercial and Administrative Law, Raising the Agency's Grades—Protecting the Economy, Assuring Regulatory Quality and Improving Assessments of Regulatory Need, 112th Cong., 1st sess., March 29, 2011, pp. 2-3, available at http://judiciary.house.gov/hearings/pdf/Glicksman03292011.pdf.

[65] Jesse Hamilton, "Dodd-Frank Rules Slow at SEC After Cost Challenge," Bloomberg, March 6, 2012, http://www.bloomberg.com/news/2012-03-06/dodd-frank-rules-slow-at-sec-after-court-cost-benefit-challenge.html.

[66] Dennis Kelleher, Stephen Hall, and Katelynn Bradley, Setting the Record Straight on Cost-Benefit Analysis and Financial Reform at the SEC, Better Markets, Inc., July 30, 2012.

[67] For two main proponents of the ossification thesis, see Thomas O. McGarity, "Some Thoughts on 'Deossifying' the Rulemaking Process," Duke Law Journal, vol. 41, no. 6 (June 1992), pp. 1385-1462; and Richard J. Pierce, Jr., "Seven Ways to Deossify Agency Rulemaking," Administrative Law Review, vol. 47, no. 1 (Winter 1995), pp. 59-98.

[68] Testimony of John D. Graham, U.S. Congress, House Committee on the Judiciary, Subcommittee on Courts, Commercial and Administrative Law, Cost-Justifying Regulations: Protecting Jobs and the Economy by Presidential and Judicial Review of Costs and Benefits, 112th Cong., 1st sess., May 4, 2011, p. 4, http://judiciary.house.gov/hearings/pdf/Graham05042011.pdf.

[69] Jason Webb Yackee and Susan Webb Yackee, "Administrative Procedures and Bureaucratic Performance: Is Federal Rule-making 'Ossified'?" Journal of Public Administration Research and Theory, vol. 20 (2010), pp. 261-282.

[70] The review process may be extended by the Director of OMB or at the request of the agency head (§ 6(b)(2)(C)).

[71] James F. Blumstein, "Regulatory Review by the Executive Office of the President: An Overview and Policy Analysis of Current Issues," Duke Law Journal, vol. 51, no. 3 (December 2001), pp. 851-899. Blumstein was nominated by President George H.W. Bush to be OIRA Administrator but was not confirmed.

[72] Testimony of Sally Katzen, U.S. Congress, House Committee on Science and Technology, Subcommittee on Investigations and Oversight, Amending Executive Order 12866: Good Governance of Regulatory Usurpation?, 110th Cong., 1st sess., February 13, 2007, p. 5, http://science.house.gov/sites/republicans.science.house.gov/files/documents/hearings/021307_katzen.pdf.

[73] Steven Croley, "White House Review of Agency Rulemaking: An Empirical Investigation," University of Chicago Law Review, vol. 70, no. 3 (Summer 2003), p. 830; and Richard H. Pildes and Cass R. Sunstein, "Reinventing the Regulatory State," University of Chicago Law Review, vol. 62, no. 1 (Winter 1995), pp. 28-33.

[74] 1 C.F.R. § 305.88-9; ACUS, Recommendation 88-9, Presidential Review of Agency Rulemaking, December 8, 1988, http://www.acus.gov/wp-content/uploads/2011/10/88-9.pdf.

[75] ABA Recommendation and Report 302, adopted by the House of Delegates August 7-8, 1990, http://www.americanbar.org/content/dam/aba/directories/policy/1990_am_302.pdf.

[76] Memorandum from the Section of Administrative Law and Regulatory Practice of the ABA to OIRA, March 16, 2009, p. 7, http://thecre.com/pdf/20090326_ABANET_comments.pdf. However, these comments noted that certain rulemaking programs should remain insulated from review, such as the regulation of political campaigns, and that "presidential oversight

may be inappropriate where 'political accountability would interfere with the successful performance of the [regulatory] function,' such as the functions performed by the Federal Reserve Board."

[77] Section of Administrative Law and Regulatory Practice, ABA, Comments on H.R. 3010, the Regulatory Accountability Act, October 24, 2011, pp. 18-19, http://www.americanbar.org content/dam/aba/administrative/ administrative_law/commentson3010_final_nocover.authcheckdam.pdf.

[78] For a summary and analysis of the controversy that arose in light of President Reagan's issuance of Executive Order 12291, see Morton Rosenberg, "Beyond the Limits of Executive Power: Presidential Control of Agency Rulemaking Under Executive Order 12,291," Michigan Law Review, vol. 80, no. 2 (December 1981), pp. 193-247.

[79] See, for example, Humphrey's Executor v. United States, 295 U.S. 602 (1935), in which the Supreme Court explained that some agencies were created by Congress to be quasi-legislative or quasi-judicial in function, by instituting "for cause" removal provisions, kept them independent of executive control.

[80] Katzen testimony, Cost Justifying Regulations, p. 8.

[81] See American Bar Association, Commission on Law and the Economy, Federal Regulation: Roads to Reform, Final Report, with Recommendations, 1979.

[82] Peter L. Strauss and Cass R. Sunstein, "The Role of the President and OMB in Informal Rulemaking," Administrative Law Review, vol. 38, no. 2 (Spring 1986), pp. 189-190.

[83] Ibid., p. 205.

[84] Katzen testimony, Cost Justifying Regulations, p. 8.

[85] Robert W. Hahn and Cass R. Sunstein, "A New Executive Order for Improving Federal Regulation? Deeper and Wider Cost-Benefit Analysis," University of Pennsylvania Law Review, vol. 150, no. 5 (May 2002), pp. 1535-1536.

[86] Testimony of Sally Katzen, U.S. Congress, House Committee on the Judiciary, Subcommittee on Courts, Commercial and Administrative Law, Cost Justifying Regulations: Protecting Jobs and the Economy by Presidential and Judicial Review of Costs and Benefits, 112th Cong., 1st sess., May 4, 2011, p. 8, http://judiciary.house.gov/hearings/ pdf/ Katzen05042011.pdf.

[87] This may explain why S. 3468 authorizes the President to issue an executive order containing requirements for CBA and centralized review, rather than creating a statutory requirement if enacted.

[88] Testimony of Peter L. Strauss, U.S. Congress, House Committee on the Judiciary, Subcommittee on Courts, Commercial, and Administrative Law, The APA at 65- Is Reform Needed to Create Jobs, Promote Economic Growth, and Reduce Costs?, 112th Cong., 1st sess., February 28, 2011, p. 6, http://judiciary.house.gov/hearings/pdf/ Strauss 02282011.pdf. Under the PRA, agencies (including IRCs) are required to seek OMB's approval of any information collection from 10 or more nonfederal persons. However, if OMB denies an information collection request from an IRC, the denial can be overturned by a majority vote of the commission's members. In that way, the PRA therefore provides limited oversight to OMB of information collections, but OMB cannot prevent one of those agencies from proceeding with such a collection.

[89] Rosenberg, "Executive Power," p. 195.

[90] See, for example, Bagley and Revesz, "Centralized Oversight," and Erik D. Olson, "The Quiet Shift of Power: Office of Management & Budget Supervision of Environmental Protection Agency Rulemaking Under Executive Order 12,291," Virginia Journal of Natural Resources Law, vol. 4, no. 1 (Fall 1984), pp. 1-80.

[91] A Washington Post article reported that OIRA's size has reduced by half over the three decades it has existed, from 90 employees to about 45, and that former OIRA officials have recommended that the agency acquire more staff. Andrew Zajac, "Regulators Surge in Numbers While Overseers Shrink," Washington Post, June 24, 2012.

[92] Testimony of David C. Vladeck, U.S. Congress, House Committee on Science and Technology, Subcommittee on Investigations and Oversight, Amending Executive Order 12866: Good Governance of Regulatory Usurpation?, 110th Cong., 1st sess., February 13, 2007, p. 4, http://science.house.gov/sites/republicans.science.house.gov/files/documents/hearings/021307_vladeck.pdf. Also see Public Citizen v. Mineta, 340 F.3d 39 (2d Cir. 2003), and Public Citizen v. FMCSA, 374 F.3d 1209 (D.C. Cir. 2004).

[93] Croley, "White House Review," p. 830.

[94] For a thorough discussion of potential enforcement actions could be taken against an IRC, including an analysis of whether the President would have the authority to remove agency officials over a disagreement in policy, see CRS Report R42720, Presidential Review of Independent Regulatory Commission Rulemaking: Legal Issues, by Vivian S. Chu and Daniel T. Shedd, pp. 16-23.

In: Independent Regulatory Commissions
Editor: Ruben Meijer

ISBN: 978-1-62808-103-9

Chapter 3

THE FEDERAL RULEMAKING PROCESS: AN OVERVIEW*

Curtis W. Copeland

SUMMARY

Federal regulation, like taxing and spending, is one of the basic tools of government used to implement public policy. Although not as frequently examined as congressional or presidential policy making, the process of developing and framing rules is viewed by some as central to the definition and implementation of public policy in the United States. Regulations generally start with an act of Congress, and are the means by which statutes are implemented and specific requirements are established. The terms "rule" or "regulation" are often used interchangeably in discussions of the federal regulatory process. The Administrative Procedure Act of 1946 defines a *rule* as "the whole or part of an agency statement of general or particular applicability and future effect designed to implement, interpret, or prescribe law or policy." The procedures that federal agencies are required to follow in writing regulations are called the rulemaking process, and are the subject of this report.

During the past 60 to 65 years, Congress and various Presidents have developed an elaborate set of procedures and requirements to guide the federal rulemaking process, often with the implicit or explicit goal of

* This is an edited, reformatted and augmented version of a Congressional Research Service publication, CRS Report for Congress RL32240, prepared for Members and Committees of Congress, from www.crs.gov, dated February 22, 2011.

reducing the amount of regulatory burden placed on the public. Statutory rulemaking requirements applicable to a wide range of agencies include the Administrative Procedure Act, the Regulatory Flexibility Act, the Paperwork Reduction Act, the Unfunded Mandates Reform Act, and the Information Quality Act. These and other cross-cutting rulemaking requirements often require some type of analysis on the part of the rulemaking agency before issuing a covered rule, but also often give agencies substantial discretion regarding whether the requirements are applicable. Other statutorily based rulemaking requirements are contained in agency- or program-specific laws, which provide varying levels of discretion regarding the substance of agencies' rules and may impose (or exclude) additional analytical or procedural requirements. The most important of the current set of presidential rulemaking requirements are in Executive Order 12866, which establishes presidential review of covered agencies' rulemaking within the Office of Management and Budget's Office of Information and Regulatory Affairs (OIRA). The executive order requires covered agencies to submit their significant rules to OIRA for review before they become final, and requires those rules to meet certain minimal standards. Other executive orders and presidential directives delineate other specific rulemaking requirements incumbent on covered agencies. However, these requirements also often provide substantial discretion to agencies regarding whether, and if so how, they are applied.

The purpose of this report is to provide Congress with an overview of the federal rulemaking process and a brief discussion of the major laws and executive orders that prescribe the procedures agencies are to apply when promulgating regulations.

INTRODUCTION

Federal regulation, like taxing and spending, is one of the basic tools of government used to implement public policy. In fact, the development and framing of a rule has been described as "the climactic act of the policy making process."[1] Another observer described the rulemaking process as "absolutely central to the definition and implementation of public policy in the United States," and said that "no significant attempt to alter the direction of a public program can succeed without effective management of the rulemaking process."[2] Regulations generally start with an act of Congress, and are the means by which statutes are implemented and specific requirements are established. Federal agencies usually issue more than 3,000 final rules each year on topics ranging from the timing of bridge openings to the permissible levels of arsenic and other contaminants in drinking water. The costs and benefits associated with all federal regulations have been a subject of great controversy, with the costs estimated in the hundreds of billions of dollars and the benefits estimates even higher. The costs federal regulations impose on regulated entities to accomplish policy goals are not reflected in the federal budget process, and some view these off-budget regulatory costs as greater than all federal domestic discretionary spending. Estimates of the benefits of federal regulations are even higher. The terms "rule" or "regulation" are often used interchangeably in discussions of the federal regulatory process. The Administrative Procedure Act (APA) of 1946 defines a rule as "the whole or part of an agency statement of general or particular applicability and future effect designed to implement, interpret, or prescribe law or policy."[3] The process by which federal agencies develop, amend, or repeal rules is called "rulemaking," and is the subject of this report.

Figure 1 illustrates in a general manner the process that most federal agencies are generally required to follow in writing or revising a significant rule. However, we should be quick to point out that some aspects of *Figure 1* do not apply to all rulemaking. For example, as discussed later in this report, an agency may, in certain circumstances, issue a final rule without issuing a notice of proposed rulemaking, thereby skipping several steps depicted in the figure. On the other hand, some rules may be published for public comment more than once. Also, independent regulatory agencies[4] are not required to submit their rules to the Office of Management and Budget's (OMB) Office of Information and Regulatory Affairs (OIRA) for review, and no agency is required to do so for rules that are not "significant."

Note at the top of *Figure 1* that the rulemaking process begins when Congress passes a statute either requiring or authorizing an agency to write and issue certain types of regulations. An initiating event (e.g., a recommendation from an outside body or a catastrophic accident) can prompt either legislation or regulation (where regulatory action has already been authorized). For example, in response to lethal chemical releases by plants in Bhopal, India, and West Virginia, Congress enacted section 313 of the Emergency Planning and Community Right-to-Know Act of 1986 (42 U.S.C. §§ 11001-11050, 11023). The act required the owners and operators of certain types of facilities to report the amounts of various toxic chemicals that the facilities release to the environment above certain thresholds, and requires the Environmental Protection Agency (EPA) to make this information available to the public. EPA subsequently issued detailed regulations implementing these requirements and, using the authority provided to it through the statute, has required reporting for more than 300 toxic substances in addition to those delineated in the law.

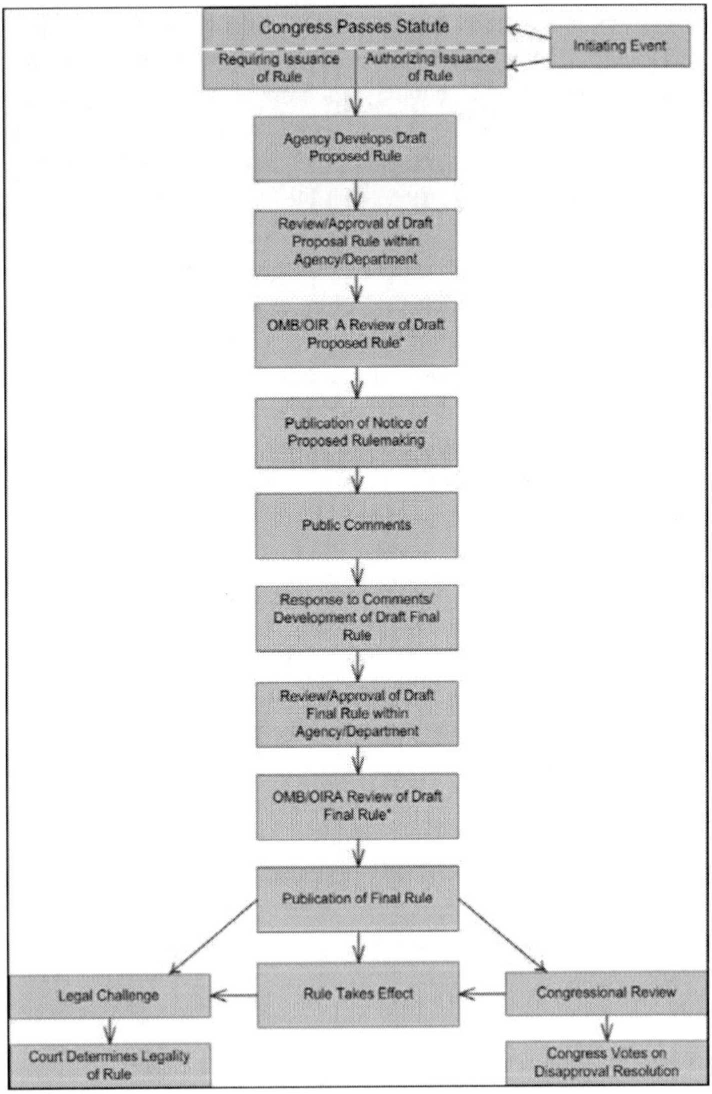

Source: CRS.

* The Office of Management and Budget's (OMB) office of Information and Regulatory Affairs (OIRA) reviews only significant rules, and does not review any rules submitted by independent regulatory agencies.

Figure 1. Federal Rulemaking Process.

As this example illustrates, the authority to regulate rests with Congress, and is delegated, through law, to an agency. The statutory basis for a regulation can vary greatly in terms of its specificity, from (1) very broad grants of authority that state only the general intent of the legislation and leave agencies with a great deal of discretion as to how that intent should be implemented, to (2) very specific requirements delineating exactly what regulatory agencies should do and how they should take action. Note also in *Figure 1* the roles that Congress and the courts can play at the end of the rulemaking process, which may result in a rule being returned to an earlier point in the process or being vacated by the reviewing body. Congress may also play a role at other stages in the process through its oversight and appropriations responsibilities.

Implicit within the steps depicted in *Figure 1* is an elaborate set of procedures and requirements that Congress and various Presidents have developed during the past 75 years to guide the federal rulemaking process. Some of these rulemaking requirements apply to virtually all federal agencies, some apply only to certain types of agencies, and others are agency-specific. Collectively, these rulemaking provisions are voluminous and require a wide range of procedural, consultative, and analytical actions on the part of rulemaking agencies. Some observers contend that the requirements have resulted in the "ossification" of the rulemaking process, causing agencies to take years to develop final rules.[5] For example, the National Advisory Committee on Occupational Safety and Health noted that it takes the Occupational Safety and Health Administration (OSHA) within the Department of Labor an average of 10 years to develop and promulgate a health or safety standard.[6] On the other hand, while these congressional and presidential rulemaking requirements are numerous, it is not clear whether they or some other factors (e.g., lack of data, congressionally imposed delays, court challenges, etc.) are the primary cause of the long time-frames that are sometimes required to develop and publish final rules.

STATUTORY RULEMAKING REQUIREMENTS

Statutory rulemaking requirements can be generally categorized into two groups—those that are specific to an individual agency or program and those that are more cross-cutting in nature, and therefore applicable to a wider range of agencies or programs. Agency- or program-specific rulemaking requirements may be in authorizing or appropriating statutes, and can have a significant or even determinative effect on an agency's rules and rulemaking procedures. As noted previously, these statutes sometimes specifically delineate what the agency's rules should require. For example, the Employee Retirement Income Security Act (29 U.S.C. § 1001 *et seq.*) gives the Pension Benefit Guaranty Corporation no discretion in drafting rules that establish minimum pension insurance premium rates, specifying to the dollar what those rates should be.[7] Also, for a number of years the Department of Transportation (DOT) concluded that it had no discretion in setting the average fuel economy standards for light trucks, and was required to keep the standard at 20.7 miles per gallon.[8] Agency-specific statutes may also impose specific procedural requirements on their rulemaking processes (e.g., the conduct of public hearings, the publication of a notice of proposed rulemaking by a particular date, or the coordination of rulemaking with another agency).

In other cases, though, the statutes give rulemaking agencies substantial discretion in how rules are developed and what they require. For example, the Agricultural Adjustment Act provides a broad grant of rulemaking authority to the Secretary of Agriculture, stating only that agricultural marketing should be "orderly" but providing little guidance regarding which crops should have marketing orders or how to apportion the market among growers.[9] More recently the Patient Protection and Affordable Care Act (PPACA, P.L. 111-148) contained a number of provisions giving federal agencies broad authority to issue "such regulations as may be necessary" to carry out certain requirements in the law.[10]

Agency rulemaking is also often significantly influenced by court decisions interpreting these agency- or program-specific statutory requirements. For example, in 1980 the Supreme Court ruled that, before promulgating new health standards, OSHA must demonstrate that the particular chemical to be regulated poses a "significant risk" under workplace conditions permitted by current regulations.[11] The court also said that OSHA must demonstrate that the new limit OSHA proposes will substantially reduce that risk. This decision effectively requires OSHA to evaluate the risks associated with exposure to a chemical and to determine that these risks are "significant" before issuing a regulatory standard. Other court decisions have required OSHA rulemaking to demonstrate the technical and economic feasibility of its requirements.[12] Still other decisions have required agencies to permit meaningful public participation in rulemaking and to fully explain what they considered and why they did and did not take particular actions.[13]

The following discussion of statutory rulemaking requirements focuses solely on the cross-cutting requirements that are applicable to more than one agency. The discussion provides descriptions of some of the major rulemaking-related statutes and is not intended to be a catalogue of all such requirements. Some of these rulemaking requirements have been in place for more than 70 years, but most have been implemented within the past 30 years. Some of these statutory requirements apply to Cabinet departments and independent agencies; others apply to those agencies as well as the independent regulatory agencies.

Federal Register Act

With the surge of New Deal legislation enacted in the 1930s, Congress made federal agencies responsible for issuing detailed regulations on a variety of complex social and economic issues. However, no central regulatory publication system existed, so there was no efficient way for citizens to know about regulations that affected them. Therefore, Congress enacted the Federal Register Act, which became law in July 1935 (44 U.S.C. Chapter 15). The act established a uniform system for handling agency regulations by requiring (1) the filing of documents with the Office of the Federal Register, (2) the placement of documents on public inspection, (3) publication of the documents in the *Federal Register*, and (4) (after a 1937 amendment) permanent codification of rules in the *Code of Federal Regulations*. Publication of a rule in the *Federal Register* provides official notice of its existence and contents. Other documents that are generally published in the *Federal Register* include presidential proclamations and executive orders, notices, and documents that the President or Congress require to be published.

Regulations for carrying out the Federal Register Act deal with, among other things, the format and distribution of the *Federal Register* and how documents are prepared, transmitted, and processed.[14] The Office of the Federal Register is responsible for printing and distributing the *Federal Register*, and the Office has published a guide and a drafting handbook explaining how *Federal Register* documents are to be prepared. The *Federal Register* is published each business day, and is now available electronically.[15]

Administrative Procedure Act

The most long-standing and broadly applicable federal rulemaking requirements are in the Administrative Procedure Act (APA) of 1946 (5

U.S.C. § 551 *et seq.*). The APA was written to bring regularity and predictability to agency decisionmaking, and provides for both formal and informal rulemaking. Formal rulemaking is used in ratemaking proceedings and in certain other cases when rules are required by statute to be made "on the record" after an opportunity for a trial-type agency hearing. However, few statutes require such on-the-record hearings. Informal rulemaking, also known as "notice and comment" rulemaking, is used much more frequently, and is the focus of this section.[16]

In informal rulemaking, the APA generally requires that agencies (Cabinet departments and independent agencies as well as independent regulatory agencies) publish a notice of proposed rulemaking (NPRM) in the *Federal Register*.[17]

The notice must contain (1) a statement of the time, place, and nature of public rulemaking proceedings; (2) reference to the legal authority under which the rule is proposed; and (3) either the terms or substance of the proposed rule or a description of the subjects and issues involved. After giving "interested persons" an opportunity to comment on the proposed rule, and after considering the public comments, the agency may then publish the final rule, incorporating a general statement of its basis and purpose. Although the APA does not specify the length of this public comment period, agencies commonly allow at least 30 days.[18] Public comments as well as other supporting materials (e.g., hearing records or agency regulatory studies but generally not internal memoranda) are placed in a rulemaking "docket" which must be available for public inspection. Finally, the APA states that the final rule cannot become effective until at least 30 days after its publication unless (1) the rule grants or recognizes an exemption or relieves a restriction, (2) the rule is an interpretative rule or a statement of policy, or (3) the agency determines that the rule should take effect sooner for good cause, and publishes that determination with the rule.

The final rule cannot adopt a provision if the NPRM did not clearly provide notice to the public that the agency was considering adopting it. If challenged in court under the APA, an agency rulemaking can be held unlawful or set aside if it is found to be "arbitrary, capricious, an abuse of discretion, or otherwise not in accordance with the law."[19] The court can also "compel agency action unlawfully withheld or unreasonably delayed." Amendment or revocation of an existing rule generally requires the responsible agency to issue a new rule through the APA process.

Exceptions to the APA Notice Requirement

Although the APA generally requires agencies to publish NPRMs before promulgating a final rule, the act provides exceptions to this requirement. For example, the APA states that the notice and comment procedures generally do not apply when an agency finds, for "good cause," that those procedures are "impracticable, unnecessary, or contrary to the public interest." When agencies use the good cause exception, the act requires that they explicitly say so and provide a rationale for the exception's use when the rule is published in the *Federal Register*. The APA also provides explicit exceptions to the NPRM requirement for certain categories of regulatory actions, such as rules dealing with military or foreign affairs; agency management or personnel; or public property, loans, grants, benefits, or contracts. Further, the APA says that the NPRM requirements do not apply to interpretative rules; general statements of policy; or rules of agency organization, procedure, or practice.[20] However, these rules do have to be published in the *Federal Register*.

The legislative history of the APA makes it clear that Congress did not believe that the act's good cause exception to the notice and comment requirements should be an "escape clause." According to the Senate committee's report accompanying the APA, a "true and supported or supportable finding of necessity or emergency must be made and published" when the agency uses the good cause exception.[21] The legislative history also indicates that Congress envisioned agencies using the notice and comment procedures even in some cases in which the APA's exceptions applied.

A federal agency's invocation of the good cause exception (or other exceptions to notice and comment procedures) is subject to judicial review. After having reviewed the totality of circumstances, the courts can and sometimes do determine that an agency's reliance on the good cause exception was not authorized under the APA.[22] The case law has generally reinforced the view that the good cause exception should be "narrowly construed."[23]

Two procedures for noncontroversial and expedited rulemaking were designed not to involve NPRMs. "Direct final" rulemaking involves agency publication of a rule in the *Federal Register* with a statement that the rule will be effective on a particular date unless an adverse comment is received within a specified period of time (e.g., 30 days). However, if an adverse comment is filed, the direct final rule is withdrawn and the agency may publish the rule as a proposed rule under normal NPRM procedures. Direct final rulemaking can be viewed as a particular application of the APA's good cause exception in which agencies claim NPRMs are "unnecessary."[24] Both Vice President Albert Gore's National Performance Review and the Administrative Conference of the United States encouraged agencies to use direct final rulemaking for noncontroversial rules.[25]

The Administrative Conference also endorsed the use of what is known as "interim final" rulemaking, in which an agency issues a final rule without an NPRM that is generally effective immediately, but with a post-promulgation opportunity for the public to comment. If the public comments persuade the agency that changes are needed in the interim final rule, the agency may revise the rule by publishing a final rule reflecting those changes. Interim final rulemaking can be viewed as another particular application of the good cause exception in the APA, but with the addition of a comment period after the rule has become effective.[26]

Congress sometimes requires agencies to use interim final rulemaking, and may also specify the length of the comment period. For example, Subsection (b)(2) of Section 1104 of the Patient Protection and Affordable Care Act amended Section 1173 of the Social Security Act (at 42 U.S.C. § 1320d-2) and states, in part, that the Secretary "shall promulgate an interim final rule applying any standard or operating rule recommended by the National Committee on Vital and Health Statistics," and "shall accept and consider public comments on any interim final rule published under this subparagraph for 60 days after the date of such publication."

In August 1998, the General Accounting Office reported that about half of the 4,658 final regulatory actions published in the *Federal Register* during 1997 were published without NPRMs.[27] Seven agencies accounted for about 70% of both the final actions and the actions without NPRMs. Most of the actions without NPRMs appeared to involve administrative or technical issues with limited applicability. However, 11 of the 61 final rules published during 1997 that were "major" (e.g., having a $100 million impact on the economy) did not have NPRMs. The agencies most commonly cited the APA's good cause exception as their justification for not publishing NPRMs, frequently noting the time-sensitive nature of the actions being taken. The agencies also frequently used the categorical exceptions permitted in the APA (e.g., actions involving agencies' management or personnel). In some cases GAO concluded that the agencies' explanations for why NPRMs were not used were not clear or understandable, with the agencies sometimes making broad assertions that an NPRM would delay the issuance of rules that were, in some general sense, in the public interest. For example, in one case the agency said that soliciting public comments on the rule was "contrary to the public interest" because the rule authorized a "new and creative method of financing the development of public housing."[28]

National Environmental Policy Act

The National Environmental Policy Act (NEPA) of 1969 (42 U.S.C. §§ 4321-4347) was the first statute to require an "impact statement" as a way to ensure that federal agencies give special consideration to certain issues during the rulemaking process. NEPA requires all federal agencies to include in every recommendation or report related to "major Federal actions significantly affecting the quality of the human environment" a detailed statement on the environmental impact of the proposed action. Initially, though, agencies make a threshold determination (known as an "environmental assessment") as to whether the rule or other action represents a significant impact on the environment. If not, the agency issues a "finding of no significant impact." If the agency concludes that there is a significant impact, the agency then prepares a full "environmental impact statement" describing the likely effects of the rule.

According to the act and its implementing regulations developed by the Council on Environmental Quality, the environmental impact statement must delineate the direct, indirect, and cumulative effects of the proposed action.[29] Agencies are also required to include in the statement (1) any adverse environmental effects that cannot be avoided should the proposal be implemented, (2) alternatives to the proposed action, (3) the relationship between local short-term uses of the environment and the maintenance and enhancement of long-term productivity, and (4) any irreversible and irretrievable commitments of resources that would be involved if the proposed action should be implemented. Before developing any such environmental impact statement, NEPA requires the responsible federal official to consult with and obtain comments of any federal agency that has jurisdiction by law or special expertise with respect to any environmental impact involved. Agencies must make copies of the statement and the comments and views of appropriate federal, state, and local agencies available to the President, the Council on Environmental Quality, and to the public. The adequacy of an agency's environmental impact statement is subject to judicial review.

In April 2002, the chairman of the Council on Environmental Quality established a task force composed of federal agency employees to review NEPA implementation practices and procedures. In September 2003, the task force issued a report containing more than 50 recommendations to expedite the NEPA review process.[30] Among other things, the task force recommended that new guidance be developed setting standards for the documentation needed to support a determination that a rule would not have significant environmental effects. Also, several pieces of legislation have been enacted since 2008 in an effort to streamline the NEPA process. [31]

Paperwork Reduction Act

The Paperwork Reduction Act (PRA) (44 U.S.C. §§ 3501-3520) was originally enacted in 1980, but was subsequently amended in 1986 and again in 1995. One of the purposes of the PRA is to minimize the paperwork burden for individuals, small businesses, and others resulting from the collection of information by or for the federal government. The act generally defines a "collection of information" as the obtaining or disclosure of facts or opinions by or for an agency by 10 or more nonfederal persons. Many information collections, recordkeeping requirements, and third-party disclosures are contained in or are authorized by regulations as monitoring or enforcement tools. In fact, these paperwork requirements are the essence of many agencies' regulatory provisions.[32] The PRA requires agencies to justify any collection of information from the public by establishing the need and intended use of the information, estimating the burden that the collection will impose on respondents, and showing that the collection is the least burdensome way to gather the information.

The original PRA established the Office of Information and Regulatory Affairs (OIRA) within the Office of Management and Budget (OMB) to provide central agency leadership and oversight of government-wide efforts to reduce unnecessary paperwork burden and improve the management of information resources. Agencies must receive OIRA approval (signified by an OMB control number displayed on the information collection) for each collection request before it is implemented, and those approvals must be renewed at least every three years. Failure to obtain OIRA approval for an active collection, or the lapse of that approval, represents a violation of the act, and triggers the PRA's public protection provision. Under that provision, no one can be penalized for failing to comply with a collection of information subject to the act if the collection does not display a valid OMB control number.[33] OIRA can disapprove any collection of information if it believes the collection is inconsistent with the requirements of the PRA.[34]

The PRA clearance process is described in the act and implementing regulations. For new collections, no later than the publication of the NPRM, the issuing agency must submit the proposed rule and any background information to OIRA. At the same time the agency is required to publish a notice in the *Federal Register* stating that OIRA's approval is being sought, thereby providing the public with an opportunity to comment on the proposed collection. For any collection of information that is not contained in a proposed rule, OIRA staff have up to 60 days under the statute to review the proposed collection and ensure, among other things, that the collection is statutorily authorized and necessary, and that the agency's paperwork burden estimate (most commonly measured in terms of "burden hours") is reasonable.[35] At the end of the process the agency is notified of the disposition of the review. OIRA data indicates that the office takes action on between 3,000 and 5,000 information collection requests (new approvals, renewals, or revisions) each year. The 1995 PRA reaffirmed the principles in the original act and gave significant new responsibilities to OIRA and executive branch agencies. For example, the act currently requires OIRA to "oversee the use of information resources to improve the efficiency and effectiveness of governmental operations to serve agency missions." The PRA also requires federal agencies to establish a process, independent of program responsibility, to evaluate proposed collections of information, manage information resources to reduce information collection burdens on the public, and ensure that the public has timely and equitable access to information products and services.

The coverage of the PRA is extremely broad, including actions by both Cabinet departments and independent agencies as well as independent regulatory agencies, and covering virtually any type of collection of information that these agencies "conduct or sponsor."[36] As a result of the 1995 amendments to the act, the PRA's clearance requirements clearly cover collections of information "requiring the disclosure to third parties or the public," effectively overturning the Supreme Court's 1990 decision in *Dole v. United Steelworkers of America* (494 U.S. 26).

One of the key features of the PRA of 1995 was the requirement that OIRA, in consultation with the agency heads, set annual government-wide goals for the reduction of information collection burdens by at least 10% in fiscal years 1996 and 1997, and by at least 5% in each of the succeeding four fiscal years. The act also required OIRA to establish agency burden reduction goals each year representing "the maximum practicable opportunity in each agency." At the end of FY1995 (just before the PRA of 1995 took effect) federal agencies estimated that their information collections imposed about 7 billion burden hours on the public. Therefore, if all federal agencies had been able to meet each of the government-wide goals, by September 30, 2001, the burden-hour estimate would have decreased about 35% to about 4.6 billion hours. However, this reduction did not occur. In fact, as of September 30,

2002, the government-wide burden estimate stood at more than 8.2 billion hours—a 17% increase since the PRA of 1995 took effect. Nearly half of that increase occurred during FY2002 alone, and about 70% occurred during fiscal years 2001 and 2002.37 The agencies contend that they are often unable to reduce paperwork requirements without changes in the underlying statutes that require the information to be collected.38 As of February 2011, there were more than 9,000 active agency information collections, with a total burden-hour estimate of nearly 9.9 billion hours.

Regulatory Flexibility Act

The Regulatory Flexibility Act (RFA) of 1980 (5 U.S.C. §§ 601-612), requires federal agencies to assess the impact of their forthcoming regulations on "small entities," which the act defines as including small businesses, small governmental jurisdictions, and certain small not-for-profit organizations. Under the RFA, Cabinet departments and independent agencies as well as independent regulatory agencies must prepare a regulatory flexibility analysis at the time proposed and certain final rules are issued. The analysis for a proposed rule is referred to as an "initial regulatory flexibility analysis" (IRFA) and the analysis for a final rule is referred to as a "final regulatory flexibility analysis." The RFA requires the analysis to describe, among other things, (1) the reasons why the regulatory action is being considered; (2) the small entities to which the proposed rule will apply and, where feasible, an estimate of their number; (3) the projected reporting, recordkeeping, and other compliance requirements of the proposed rule; and (4) any significant alternatives to the rule that would accomplish the statutory objectives while minimizing the impact on small entities.[39]

However, these analytical requirements are not triggered if the head of the issuing agency certifies that the proposed rule would not have a "significant economic impact on a substantial number of small entities." The RFA does not define "significant economic impact" or "substantial number of small entities," thereby giving federal agencies substantial discretion regarding when the act's analytical requirements are initiated. Also, the RFA's analytical requirements do not apply to final rules for which the agency does not publish a proposed rule.[40] The RFA initially did not permit judicial review of agencies' actions under the act. However, amendments to the act in 1996 as part of the Small Business Regulatory Enforcement Fairness Act (SBREFA) (110 Stat. 857, 5 U.S.C. § 601 note) permitted judicial review regarding, among other things, agencies' regulatory flexibility analyses for final rules and any certifications that their rules will not have a significant impact on small entities. As a result, a small entity that is adversely affected or aggrieved by an agency's determination that its final rule would not have a significant impact on small entities could seek judicial review of that determination within one year of the date of the final agency action. In granting relief, a court may remand the rule to the agency or defer enforcement against small entities. The addition of judicial review in 1996 is generally viewed as a significant strengthening of the RFA, and is believed to have improved agencies' compliance with the act.[41]

The RFA also contains several other notable provisions. For example, section 602 requires each federal agency to publish a "regulatory flexibility agenda" in the *Federal Register* each October and April listing regulations that the agency expects to propose or promulgate which are likely to have a significant economic impact on a substantial number of small entities.[42] Section 610 of the act requires agencies to review those rules that have or will have a significant impact within 10 years of their promulgation to determine whether they should be continued without change or should be amended or rescinded to minimize their impact on small entities. Section 612 of the RFA requires the Chief Counsel of the Small Business Administration's (SBA) Office of Advocacy to monitor and report at least annually on agencies' compliance with the act. SBA's primary method of monitoring agencies' compliance is to review and comment on proposed regulations when they are published for notice and comment in the *Federal Register*. However, the statute also specifically authorizes the Chief Counsel to appear as *amicus curiae* (i.e., "friend of the court") in any court action to review a rule.

The RFA also requires agencies to ensure that small entities have an opportunity to participate in the rulemaking process, and the 1996 amendments to the act in SBREFA put in place special requirements for proposed rules issued by the Environmental Protection Agency (EPA) and the Occupational Safety and Health Administration (OSHA). The Dodd-Frank Wall Street Reform and Consumer Protection Act (P.L. 111-203) required the new Consumer Financial Protection Bureau (CFPB) to also hold such panels. EPA , OSHA, and CFPB are required to convene "advocacy review panels" before publishing a regulatory flexibility analysis for a proposed rule. Specifically, the agency issuing the regulation must notify the SBA Chief Counsel for Advocacy and provide information on the draft rule's potential impacts on small entities and the type of small entities that might be affected. The Chief Counsel then must identify representatives of affected small entities within 15 days of the notification. The review panel must consist of full-time federal employees from the rulemaking agency, the Office of Management and Budget, and SBA's Chief Counsel for Advocacy. During the panel process, the panel must collect the advice and recommendations of representatives of affected small entities about the potential impact of the draft rule. The panel must report on the comments received and on the panel's recommendations no later than 60 days after the panel is convened, and the panel's report must be made public as part of the rulemaking record.[43] The agency may or may not adopt the panel's recommendations. GAO has examined the implementation of the RFA several times within the past 10 to 15 years, and a recurring theme in GAO's reports is a lack of clarity in the act and a resulting variability in the act's implementation. For example, in 1991 GAO reported that each of the four federal agencies that it reviewed had a different interpretation of key RFA provisions.[44] In 1994 GAO again reported that agencies' compliance with the RFA varied widely from one agency to another and that agencies were interpreting the statute differently.[45] In a 1999 report on the implementation of section 610 of the RFA and in a 2000 report on the implementation of the RFA at the Environmental Protection Agency (EPA), GAO concluded that agencies had broad discretion to determine what the statute required.[46] In all of these reports, GAO suggested that Congress consider clarifying the act's requirements and/or give SBA or some other entity the responsibility to develop criteria for whether and how agencies should conduct RFA analyses. In 2001, GAO testified that the promise of the RFA may never be realized until Congress or some other entity defines what a "significant economic impact" and a "substantial number of small entities" mean in a rulemaking setting.[47] However, other observers have indicated that the definitions of these terms should remain flexible because of significant differences in each agency's operating environment.

Periodically, legislation is introduced to amend the RFA. For example, in the 112th Congress, H.R. 527, the Regulatory Flexibility Improvements Act of 2011, would (among other things) clarify and expand the rules covered by the act, and require the SBA Chief Counsel for Advocacy to "issue rules governing agency compliance with this chapter."[48]

Small Business Regulatory Enforcement Fairness Act

As noted in the previous section of this report, certain provisions in SBREFA amended the RFA to permit judicial review and to permit small entities to participate in EPA and OSHA rulemaking before a proposed rule with a significant impact on small entities is published. Other provisions in SBREFA did not amend the RFA, but imposed new rulemaking-related requirements on federal agencies.

For example, section 212 of SBREFA requires agencies to develop one or more compliance guides for each final rule or group of related final rules for which the agency is required to prepare a regulatory flexibility analysis. Specifically, section 212 requires the guides to (1) be published, (2) be designated as "small entity compliance guides," and (3) explain the actions a small entity is required to take to comply with an associated final rule. However, the discretion inherent in the RFA regarding when a regulatory flexibility analysis is required also applies to whether compliance guides must be developed. Section 212 gives agencies broad discretion in other areas as well. For example, it says agencies "may" prepare separate guides covering groups or classes of similarly affected small entities, and "may" cooperate with associations of small entities to develop and distribute the guides. Agencies are given "sole discretion" in the use of plain language in the guides. The statute does not indicate when the guides must be developed or how they must be "published." In December 2001, GAO reported that section 212 of SBREFA did not appear to have had much of an impact on agencies' rulemaking activities, and its implementation varied across and sometimes within agencies.[49] Using the discretion that the section provided, GAO said "an agency could legally exclude all of its rules from coverage by the statute, designate a previously published document as its small entity compliance guide, or develop and publish a guide with no input from small entities years after the covered rule takes effect." GAO recommended several changes it felt were needed to strengthen and clarify the requirements in section 212.[50]

Section 213 of SBREFA required federal agencies regulating the activities of small entities to establish a program for responding to inquiries concerning compliance with applicable statutes and regulations. The section also says that in any civil or administrative action against a small entity, such guidance "may be considered as evidence of the reasonableness or appropriateness of any proposed fines, penalties or damages sought against such small entity."

Section 222 of SBREFA amended the Small Business Act (15 U.S.C. §631 *et seq.*) to require the SBA Administrator to designate a "Small Business and Agriculture Regulatory Enforcement Ombudsman," who was directed to work with each agency to ensure that small business concerns have an opportunity to comment on agencies' enforcement actions. The ombudsman was directed to annually evaluate and report on each agency's enforcement activities, including a rating of the "responsiveness to small business" of each agency's regional and program offices. Section 222 also required the Administrator to establish a "Small Business Regulatory Fairness Board" in each SBA regional office to report to and advise the ombudsman on "excessive enforcement actions of agencies against small business concerns.

Section 223 of SBREFA requires agencies to provide small entities with some form of relief from civil monetary penalties. Specifically, subsection 223(a) of the act required federal agencies regulating the activities of small entities to establish a policy or program by end of March 1997 for the reduction and, under appropriate circumstances, the waiver of civil penalties by small entities. In February 2001, GAO reported on the implementation of section 223 and concluded that all of the agencies' penalty reduction and waiver policies were within the broad discretion afforded by the statute.[51] However, GAO also reported that some of the policies covered only a portion of the agencies' enforcement actions involving small entities, and some treated small entities no differently than large entities. The agencies' policies also differed in terms of how key terms such as "small entity" and "penalty reduction" were defined, and most were developed before SBREFA took effect. GAO suggested several changes to the statute to strengthen agencies' penalty relief policies and make them more consistent. For example, GAO suggested amending the act to require agencies to maintain data on the number of enforcement actions involving small entities and the amount of penalty relief provided. This recommendation was later implemented with the passage of the Small Business Paperwork Relief Act of 2002 (P.L. 107-198, 116 Stat. 729), which required (among other things) that agencies develop and report such information to selected congressional committees.

Congressional Review Act

The statutory provision commonly known as the Congressional Review Act (CRA) (5 U.S.C. §§ 801-808) was included as part of SBREFA as enacted in March 1996, and established expedited procedures by which Congress may disapprove agencies' rules by enacting a joint resolution of disapproval.[52] Under the CRA, before any final rule can become effective it must be filed with each house of Congress and GAO.[53] The act also requires federal agencies to submit to GAO and make available to each house of Congress a copy of any cost-benefit analysis prepared for the rule and a report on the agency's actions related to the RFA and any other relevant act or executive order. The definition of a "rule" under the CRA is very broad, and the act applies to rules issued by Cabinet departments and independent agencies as well as independent regulatory agencies.

If OIRA considers the issuing agency's rule to be "major" (e.g., has a $100 million effect on the economy), the agency generally must delay the rule's effective date by 60 days after the date of publication in the *Federal Register* or submission to Congress and GAO, whichever is later. Within 15 calendar days of receiving a major rule, GAO is required to provide Congress with a report on the rule assessing the issuing agency's compliance with the procedural steps required by the various acts and executive orders applicable to the rulemaking process.[54] Although the CRA establishes these special requirements for major rules, the CRA procedures for disapproving regulations apply to all rules, whether or not they are declared to be major.

Within 60 days after Congress receives an agency's rule, excluding periods when Congress is in recess or adjournment, a Member of Congress can introduce a resolution of disapproval that, if adopted by both Houses and enacted into law, can nullify the rule, even if it has already gone into effect. Congressional disapproval under the CRA also prevents the agency from proposing to issue a "substantially similar" rule without subsequent statutory authorization, but this provision is not intended to vitiate altogether the agency's power to establish regulations in the area in question.

The CRA provides that Senate action on a disapproval resolution under the act must occur within 60 days of session after the regulation is submitted, and makes available during that period an expedited procedure intended to ensure that the Senate can take up and vote on the measure before the period expires. The act establishes no such expedited procedure for the House. If Congress adjourns less than 60 days of session after a rule is submitted, a new 60 day period for disapproval under the act begins on the 15th legislative day of the next session. If a disapproval resolution is rejected by either house of Congress, the rule can take effect immediately (or as provided by other governing law or rule).

Federal agencies have submitted more than 50,000 rules to GAO (and presumably, Congress) since the CRA took effect in March 1996, including more than 1,000 major rules. However, only one rule had been overturned through CRA's procedures—OSHA's ergonomics standard in March 2001 (P.L. 107-5). Many reasons have been suggested for why the CRA has not been used more often,[55] but chief among them may be the fact that, if the President vetoes a resolution of disapproval (which is likely if the underlying rule is developed during his administration), then enactment of the resolution would require approval of a two-thirds majority in both houses of Congress. The rejection of the ergonomics rule was the result of a specific set of circumstances created by a transition in party control of the presidency. The majority party in both houses of Congress was the same as the party of the incoming President (George W. Bush). When the new Congress convened in 2001 and adopted a resolution disapproving the rule published under the outgoing President (William J. Clinton), the incoming President did not veto the resolution. Congress may be most able to use the CRA to disapprove rules in similar, transition-related circumstances.[56]

Congress can also stop agency rulemaking or regulatory enforcement through provisions added to agency appropriations legislation. There appear to be four types of such appropriations provisions: (1) restrictions on the finalization of particular proposed rules, (2) restrictions on regulatory activity within certain areas, (3) implementation or enforcement restrictions, and (4) conditional restrictions (e.g., preventing implementation of a rule until certain actions are taken). Some of these kinds of provisions have been included in appropriations bills for many years in a row. The reasons behind these restrictions vary, with some appearing to be based on economic considerations, some requiring or preventing the implementation of rules issued at the end of a presidential administration, and some included for various other reasons. Such provisions are generally applicable only for the period of time and the agencies covered by the relevant appropriations bill, but (depending on how they are worded) can be more broadly applicable. Also, to the extent that agencies have independent sources of funding (e.g., user fees) or implement their regulations through state or local governments, some of the limitations may not be as restrictive as they seem.[57]

Unfunded Mandates Reform Act

The Unfunded Mandates Reform Act (UMRA) of 1995 was enacted in an effort to reduce the costs associated with federal imposition of responsibilities, duties, and regulations upon state, local, and tribal governments and the private sector without providing the funding appropriate to the costs imposed by those responsibilities. Title I of UMRA established new procedures designed to ensure that Congress fully considers the potential effects of unfunded federal mandates before imposing them in legislation. Among other things, the procedures call for the Congressional Budget Office to provide statements to authorizing committees about whether reported bills contain mandates and, if so, the cost of those mandates.[58]

Title II of UMRA (2 U.S.C. §§ 1532-1538) contains requirements imposed on covered federal agencies during the rulemaking process. Specifically, the act requires Cabinet departments and independent agencies (but not independent regulatory agencies) to, among other things:

- prepare a written statement containing specific descriptions and estimates for any proposed rule or any final rule for which a proposed rule was published that includes any federal mandate that may result in the expenditure of $100 million or more in any year by state, local, or tribal governments, in the aggregate, or the private sector. One of the items required in the written statement is a qualitative and quantitative assessment of the anticipated costs and benefits of the mandate (Section 202);
- identify and consider a reasonable number of regulatory alternatives and select the least costly, most cost-effective, or least burdensome alternative (or explain why that alternative was not selected) for each rule for which a written statement is prepared (Section 205);
- develop a plan in which agencies provide notice of regulatory requirements to potentially affected small governments (Section 203); and
- develop an effective process to permit elected officers of state, local, and tribal governments (or their designees) to provide input in the development of regulatory proposals containing significant intergovernmental mandates (Section 204).

OIRA has primary responsibility for monitoring agency compliance with title II of UMRA, and issued guidance in March 1995 on the implementation of the title that generally repeated the requirements of the statute. OIRA also publishes an annual report on the implementation of title II.[59]

In February 1998, GAO reported that, because of the way the statute was written, title II of UMRA had little effect on agencies' rulemaking actions during its first two years of implementation.[60] First, many of the act's requirements did not appear to apply to most of the "economically significant" rules (e.g., rules with a $100 million impact on the economy) that were promulgated during this period. For example, if a final rule did not have an associated NPRM or imposed a mandate as a condition of federal financial assistance, the written statement requirement in section 202 of UMRA does not apply. Second, UMRA does not require agencies to take the actions specified if the agencies determine that they are duplicative of other actions or that accurate estimates of the effect of their rules are not feasible. Third, even when UMRA is triggered, it often requires agencies to take actions that are identical or similar to actions that they were already required to take. For example, UMRA's requirements in sections 202 and 205 for the conduct of cost-benefit analysis and identification of regulatory alternatives are similar to the requirements that were already in place under Executive Order 12866, which was issued more than a year before UMRA was enacted. (See below for a discussion of "Executive Order 12866.") The consultation requirements in section 204 are traceable to the notice and comment requirements in the APA, and are almost identical to the requirements in Executive Order 12875, which was issued more than a year before UMRA.

In May 2004, GAO again reported that UMRA's written statement requirements did not apply to most major or economically significant final rules issued in 2001 and 2002 (only 9 of 122).[61] However, GAO also said that some of the rules not triggering UMRA's requirements "appeared to have potential financial impacts on affected nonfederal parties similar to those of the actions that were identified as containing mandates at or above the act's thresholds." In March 2005, GAO reported that parties from various sectors (businesses, public interest groups, academia, and others) most commonly cited UMRA's numerous definitions, exclusions, and exceptions as problematic and in need of improvement.[62] In February 2011, GAO reiterated these conclusions, noting that there are 14 reasons why a rule would not be considered a "mandate" under UMRA.[63]

Information Quality Act

Section 515 of the Treasury and General Government Appropriations Act for Fiscal Year 2001, generally known as the "Data Quality Act" or the "Information Quality Act" (IQA) amended the Paperwork Reduction Act and directed OMB to issue government-wide guidelines that "provide policy and procedural guidance to Federal agencies for ensuring and maximizing the quality, objectivity, utility, and integrity of information (including statistical information) disseminated by Federal agencies."[64] The IQA also instructed agencies (both Cabinet departments and independent agencies as well as independent regulatory agencies) to issue their own guidelines not more than one year after the issuance of OMB's government-wide guidelines, and to establish administrative mechanisms allowing affected persons to seek and obtain correction of information maintained and disseminated by the agency. Finally, the act required agencies to report periodically to the Director of OMB on the number and nature of complaints received and how such complaints were handled by the agency. The first agency reports were due by January 1, 2004.

In response to a separate congressional requirement, in April 2004, OMB provided Congress with a report on the implementation of the IQA during FY2003.[65] The report said that agencies received only about 35 substantive correction requests during the year, and said it was "premature to make broad statements about both the impact of the correction request process and the overall responsiveness of the agencies." Many other correction requests listed in the report were on minor issues or involved matters that had been dealt with before the IQA was enacted. OMB indicated that the correction requests came from all segments of society, and said there was no evidence that the IQA had affected the pace of rulemaking. However, OMB Watch (a public interest group) said OMB's report was "seriously flawed" in that it understated the number of correction requests and did not disclose that nearly three-quarters of the requests were from industry.[66]

The IQA builds upon existing agency responsibilities to assure the quality of information collected, used, or disseminated to the public. Proponents of the act contend that the law and the OMB and agency guidelines will improve the quality of agency science and regulation, and force agencies to regulate based on the best science available. Some of these proponents also maintain that the act will help agencies defend their regulations against lawsuits and reduce the number of lawsuits filed. They also point out that in any requests for correction of information, the IQA places the burden of proof on the affected parties making the request; they must demonstrate that a specific dissemination does not meet the standards of either the OMB guidelines or the agency-specific guidelines. However, opponents of the act and the guidelines contend the IQA may have a chilling effect on agency distribution and use of scientific information. These opponents foresee a flood of information quality challenges, correction requests, and court suits on a wide range of scientific issues, which may tie up agency resources and significantly delay health, safety, and environmental regulations. Opponents have also noted that since "quality" is a subjective term and some regulations are based on "best available data," regulations could be arbitrarily rejected under this new law.

A major test of the IQA concerned whether agencies' denials of information correction requests are subject to judicial review. In March 2006, the U.S. Court of Appeals for the Fourth Circuit ruled that the act does not permit judicial review.[67] Two district courts had previously reached a similar conclusion,[68] and the Department of Justice had issued a brief stating that the IQA does not permit judicial review.[69]

Peer Review

In a development closely related to the issue of information quality, in September 2003, OMB published a proposed bulletin on "Peer Review and Information Quality" that would have, if made final, provided a standardized process by which all significant regulatory information would be peer reviewed.[70] The authorities that OMB cited for this action were the IQA, the Paperwork Reduction Act, and Executive Order 12866. "Regulatory information" was defined in the bulletin as any scientific or technical study that "might" be used by federal, state, local, or international regulatory bodies.

Specifically, the bulletin proposed requiring each federal agency (each executive agency and independent regulatory agency) to take three actions: (1) have all "significant regulatory information" that it intends to disseminate peer reviewed (with information defined as "significant" if OMB determines that it will have a clear and substantial impact on important public policies or private sector decisions); (2) have "especially significant regulatory information" subject to the above requirements peer reviewed according to even higher standards (with information deemed "especially significant" if, among other things, it supports a regulatory action with a $100 million or more impact on the economy or "is relevant to an Administration policy priority"); and (3) provide OMB at least once each year with information about upcoming significant regulatory disseminations and the agency's plans for conducting peer reviews. The proposed bulletin also said agencies that are likely to disseminate "significant" or "especially significant" regulatory information must supplement or amend their information quality guidelines to incorporate the requirements of the proposed peer review bulletin for "significant" and "especially significant" information. The proposed bulletin indicated that OMB could waive the requirements for peer review if an agency made "a compelling case" that a waiver is necessary (e.g., an imminent health hazard or homeland security threat). OMB received 187 comments from the public and other agencies on its proposed peer review bulletin, with some supporting its issuance in final and others calling for its withdrawal and reconsideration. On April 15, 2004, OMB published a revised bulletin, and again asked the public for comments.[71]

On December 15, 2004, OMB published a final version of the peer review bulletin on its website.[72] The final bulletin was published in the *Federal Register* on January 14, 2005.[73] OMB said this version reflects "minor revisions" made in response to more than 50 comments from the public on the revised bulletin. For example, the final bulletin requires agencies to disclose the names of peer reviewers to the public and adds an annual reporting requirement to allow OMB to track how agencies are using the bulletin. However, agencies are still afforded substantial discretion to determine when and what type of peer review is required. OMB also retains substantial discretion in certain areas.

OMB and supporters of the peer review bulletin indicate that peer review standards across the government are currently inconsistent, and that more consistent use of peer review can increase the technical quality and credibility of regulatory science.[74] They also assert that peer review can protect science-based regulations from political criticism and litigation. Opponents view the bulletin as an effort to inject political considerations into the world of science and to use the uncertainty that inevitably surrounds science as an excuse to delay new rules that could cost regulated entities millions or even billions of dollars. They also expressed concerns regarding the need for the bulletin and OMB's authority to issue it.[75]

Other Statutory Provisions Related to Rulemaking

Other statutory provisions have been enacted over the years that, while generally not imposing new rulemaking requirements per se, can affect the rulemaking process.

Federal Advisory Committee Act

Several statutes either require or permit the use of advisory committees in the federal rulemaking process. An advisory committee may be composed of experts in the regulatory field involved, representatives of the interest groups affected by the rule, and related federal or state agencies, and may help set the agency's rulemaking agenda or may simply serve as a sounding board for agency ideas. The enactment of the Federal Advisory Committee Act (FACA) of 1972 (5 U.S.C. App. II) established requirements to ensure that agencies using advisory committees receive impartial and relevant expertise. Specifically, FACA requires that the advice provided by advisory committees be objective and accessible to the public. With certain exceptions, each advisory committee meeting is presumptively open to the public. Adequate advance notice of the meetings must be published in the *Federal Register*, and all papers, records, and minutes of the meetings must generally be made available to the public. FACA also requires that the advisory committees be fairly balanced in regard to the points of view of affected interests and the functions performed. The act defines an advisory committee as any committee or similar group (1) established or used to obtain advice or recommendation for one or more federal agencies or the President and (2) that is not composed wholly of full-time federal officers or employees.[76]

Trade Agreements Act

The Trade Agreements Act of 1979 (19 U.S.C. §§ 2531-2533) prohibits agencies from setting regulatory standards that create "unnecessary obstacles to foreign commerce" of the United States. The act specifically states that legitimate domestic objectives such as safety or health are not considered unnecessary obstacles.

The statute also requires, where appropriate, the use of performance standards rather than design standards and the consideration of international standards as the basis of domestic standards.

Negotiated Rulemaking Act

The Negotiated Rulemaking Act of 1990 (5 U.S.C. §§ 561-570a), as amended and permanently authorized in 1996 (110 Stat. 3870), seeks to overcome what some observers describe as an adversarial relationship between agencies and affected interest groups that often accompanies agency rulemaking. The concept of negotiated rulemaking (sometimes referred to as regulatory negotiation or "reg-neg") emerged in the 1980s as a supplement to the traditional procedure for developing regulations. Negotiated rulemaking does not replace procedures necessary under the APA. Instead, the act encourages (but does not require) agencies to consider convening a negotiated rulemaking committee before developing and issuing a proposed regulation under the APA. The committee, composed of representatives of the agency and the various interest groups that would be affected by the proposed regulation, addresses areas of concern in the hope that it can reach agreement on the contents of a proposed regulation. The agency can, if it agrees, then issue the agreement as a proposed rule, and eventually a final rule under existing APA requirements. The expectation is that any rule drafted through negotiated rulemaking would be easier to implement and less likely to be the subject of subsequent litigation. However, any proposal agreed to by the negotiated rulemaking committee is not binding on the agency or other parties.

The major provisions of the act require that (1) a negotiated rulemaking committee consist of at least one member of the agency and no more than 25 members, unless the head of the agency determines that more are needed; (2) the agency select an impartial "facilitator" to chair meetings, subject to the approval of the committee by consensus; (3) an agreement on any negotiated rulemaking must be unanimous, unless the negotiated rulemaking committee agrees to other conditions; and (4) the head of an agency, when deciding whether to establish a negotiated rulemaking committee, assure that (a) there are a limited number of identifiable interests that will be significantly affected by the rule; (b) there is a reasonable chance that a committee can be convened with a balanced representation of interested parties willing to negotiate in good faith; and (c) there is a reasonable likelihood that a committee will reach a consensus on the proposed rule within a fixed period of time.

An agency may pay reasonable travel and *per diem* expenses, and reasonable compensation to negotiating committee members under certain conditions.

The agency must comply with FACA in establishing and administering the committee. Agency procedural actions related to establishing, assisting, or terminating the committee are not subject to judicial review, but any judicial review available regarding the rule resulting from negotiated rulemaking is unaffected.[77]

Although the use of negotiated rulemaking was expected to improve rulemaking timeliness and reduce litigation, one examination of agencies' efforts in this area indicated that those expectations were not being fulfilled.[78] However, another study indicated that negotiated rulemaking can improve participants' perception of the final rule and of the overall rulemaking process.[79]

Although the Negotiated Rulemaking Act gives agencies substantial discretion as to whether the approach should be employed in rulemaking, Congress has sometimes mandated its use by rulemaking agencies and established specific procedures and time frames to follow. For example, Section 5602 of the Patient Protection and Affordable Care Act requires the Secretary of Health and Human Services to use negotiated rulemaking to establish a "comprehensive methodology and criteria for designation of ... (A) medically underserved populations in accordance with section 330(b)(3) of the Public Health Service Act (42 U.S.C. § 254b(b)(3))," and "(B) health professions shortage areas under section 332 of the Public Health Service Act (42 U.S.C. § 254e)."[80]

National Technology Transfer and Advancement Act

Section 12(d) of the National Technology Transfer and Advancement Act (15 U.S.C. § 272 note), adopted in March 1996, generally requires federal agencies to "use technical standards that are developed or adopted by voluntary consensus standards bodies" to carry out policy objectives unless doing so is "inconsistent with applicable law or otherwise impractical." Agencies are also required to consult with and (if in the public interest and compatible with agency missions, authority, priorities, and resources) participate with voluntary, private sector, consensus bodies. This provision essentially codified policies already in existence in OMB Circular A-119, and also established reporting requirements and authorized the National Institute of Standards and Technology (NIST) within the Department of Commerce to coordinate agencies' conformity assessment activities. According to NIST, federal agencies use consensus standards in hundreds of federal procurement or regulatory programs (e.g., requiring certification from Underwriters Laboratories that a product is safe or requiring individuals in certain professions meet specific educational or competency standards).[81]

Regulatory Right-to-Know Act

Section 624 of the Treasury and General Government Appropriations Act, 2001 (31 U.S.C. § 1105 note), sometimes referred to as the "Regulatory Right-to-Know Act," requires OMB to prepare and submit with the budget an "accounting statement and associated report" containing an estimate of the total costs and benefits (including quantifiable and nonquantifiable effects) of federal rules and paperwork, to the extent feasible, (1) in the aggregate, (2) by agency and agency program, and (3) by major rule. The accounting statement is also to contain an analysis of impacts of federal regulation on state, local, and tribal governments, small businesses, wages, and economic growth. The statute requires an accounting statement and report for calendar year 2002 "and each year thereafter."[82] To prepare the report, OMB relies heavily on agencies' estimates of costs and benefits for individual rules published during the previous 10 years. However, if an agency quantified but did not monetize its estimates, OMB monetizes them using "standard" assumptions. In its reports, OMB attempts to capture the agencies' nonquantified benefits and costs in "other information" columns, but OMB's monetized estimates exclude these effects.[83]

Government Paperwork Elimination Act

In 1998, Congress enacted the Government Paperwork Elimination Act (GPEA) (44 U.S.C. § 3504 note), which required that by October 21, 2003, federal agencies provide the public, when practicable, with the option of submitting, maintaining, and disclosing information electronically, instead of on paper. GPEA makes OMB responsible for ensuring that federal agencies meet the act's implementation deadline. Although GPEA does not specifically mention rulemaking, both OMB and rulemaking agencies have indicated that its requirements have provided an impetus for developing information technology-based approaches to rulemaking that involves information collection and, more generally, to regulatory management.

E-Government Act

The E-Government Act of 2002 (44 U.S.C.A. § 3601 note) was designed to enhance the management and promotion of electronic government services and processes, and contains requirements affecting the rulemaking process. Specifically, section 206 of the act requires agencies, to the extent practicable, to:

- ensure that a publicly accessible website includes all information about that agency that is required to be published in the *Federal Register*,
- accept public comments on proposed rules "by electronic means," and
- ensure that a publicly accessible federal website contains "electronic dockets" for proposed rules containing all comments submitted on the rules as well as "other materials that by agency rule or practice are included in the rulemaking docket under (the APA), whether or not submitted electronically."

The E-Government Act also requires agencies to conduct a "privacy impact assessment" before initiating a new collection of information that uses information technology and contains individually identifying information. In addition, the act established an Office of Electronic Government within OMB, headed by an Administrator appointed by the President. It requires the Administrator of that office to work with the Administrator of OIRA in establishing the strategic direction of the e-government program, and to oversee its implementation.

In January 2003, the Bush Administration launched the "Regulations.gov" website—the first module of its own "e-rulemaking" initiative that would accomplish many of the objectives of the E-Government Act. The website permits the public to identify proposed rules that are open for comment government-wide, and permits the public to comment electronically on those rules.[84] The second module of the e-rulemaking initiative is intended to create one or more electronic dockets for proposed and final rules. The Environmental Protection Agency (EPA) is the lead agency for the e-rulemaking initiative.

E-rulemaking has been described as a way to increase democratic legitimacy, improve regulatory policy decisions, decrease administrative costs, and increase regulatory compliance. However, the implementation of e-rulemaking in the federal government has been controversial. Although the migration of agencies into the government-wide docket was originally planned for 2004, that migration was not completed until 2008. Congress has objected to how e-rulemaking and several other e-government projects have been funded (through appropriations transfers or reimbursements to the projects' "managing partner" agencies), and has voiced other concerns about the overall management and appropriateness of the initiatives. Questions have also been raised regarding the e-rulemaking initiative's centralized structure, its costs (more than $53 million spent through FY2008) and expected financial benefits, the functionality of some of the applications being used, and its effect on public participation in the rulemaking process.

The reasons why the federal e-rulemaking initiative had such a difficult first five years are many, but one appears to be the lack of direct, consistent funding. From FY2003 through FY2007, Congress appropriated less than $20 million to the E-Government Fund for all e-government projects—much less than the $345 million authorized in the E-Government Act for that period. Congress has also required approval by the Appropriations Committees before any transfers or reimbursements of appropriations are made. Although some have suggested that better communication is needed between Congress and the executive branch, the conflicts may reflect basic differences of opinion between the two branches regarding control of federal operations and how the branches should interact. A long-term issue is whether e-rulemaking should continue to be housed in EPA.[85]

Small Business Paperwork Relief Act

In June 2002, Congress enacted and the President signed the Small Business Paperwork Relief Act of 2002 (P.L. 107-198). The act amended the Paperwork Reduction Act to, among other things, require each agency to establish a single point of contact to act as a liaison for small business concerns with regard to information collection and paperwork issues. It also directed agencies to make a special effort to reduce information collection burdens for small businesses with fewer than 25 employees. OMB was directed to publish in the *Federal Register* and make available on the Internet an annual list of the compliance assistance resources available to small businesses.[86] The act also required agencies to report to Congress on the amount of penalty relief provided to small businesses, and established a task force to study the feasibility of streamlining information collection requirements on small businesses.

EXECUTIVE ORDERS AND DIRECTIVES

During the past 20 years, each President has issued executive orders and/or presidential directives designed to guide the federal rulemaking process, often with the goal of reducing regulatory burden. Although independent regulatory agencies are generally not covered by these requirements, they are often encouraged to follow them. By far the most important of the current executive rulemaking requirements is Executive Order 12866,[87] which describes both the principles and the process by which presidential regulatory review currently takes place.

Executive Order 12866

Centralized review of agencies' regulations within the Executive Office of the President has been part of the federal rulemaking process for more than 30 years. Although each of his three predecessors had some type of review process, the most significant development in the evolution of presidential review of rulemaking occurred in 1981, when President Reagan issued Executive Order 12291. The executive order established a set of general requirements for rulemaking, and required federal agencies (other than independent regulatory agencies) to send a copy of each draft proposed and final rule to OMB before publication in the *Federal Register*. It also required covered agencies to prepare a regulatory impact analysis for each "major" rule (e.g., those with a $100 million impact on the economy). As a result of this order, OIRA's responsibilities were greatly expanded from paperwork reviews to examinations of the substance of covered agencies rules—between 2,000 and 3,000 reviews per year. In 1985, President Reagan expanded OIRA's influence further by issuing Executive Order 12498, which required covered agencies (all except independent regulatory agencies) to submit a regulatory plan to OMB for review each year that covered all of their significant regulatory actions underway or planned.

On September 30, 1993, President Clinton issued Executive Order 12866, which revoked Executive Orders 12291 and 12498 and established a new process for OIRA review of rules.[88] Like its predecessors, the new executive order limited OIRA's reviews to proposed and final rules published by agencies other than independent regulatory agencies. However, it also limited OIRA reviews to actions identified by the rulemaking agency or OIRA as "significant" regulatory actions, defined as those that were "economically significant" (e.g., those with a $100 million impact on the economy) or that (1) were inconsistent or interfered with an action taken or planned by another agency; (2) materially altered the budgetary impact of entitlements, grants, user fees, or loan programs; or (3) raised novel legal or policy issues. As a result, the number of rules that OIRA reviewed dropped from between 2,000 and 3,000 per year to between 500 and 700 per year.

Executive Order 12866 also differs from its predecessors in other respects. For example, the order requires that OIRA generally complete its reviews of proposed and final rules within 90 calendar days. It also requires both rulemaking agencies and OIRA to disclose certain information about how the regulatory reviews were conducted. For example, agencies are to identify for the public (1) the substantive changes made to rules between the draft submitted to OIRA for review and the action subsequently announced, and (2) changes made at the suggestion or recommendation of OIRA. OIRA is required to, among other things, provide agencies with a copy of all communications between OIRA personnel and parties outside of the executive branch, and to maintain a public log of all regulatory actions under review and of all of the documents provided to the agencies.[89]

For each significant draft rule, the executive order requires the issuing agency to provide to OIRA the text of the draft rule, a description of why the rule is needed, and a general assessment of the rule's costs and benefits. For draft rules that are "economically significant," the executive order requires a detailed cost-benefit analysis, including an assessment of the costs and benefits of "potentially effective and reasonably feasible alternatives to the planned regulation." One of the "principles of regulation" in the order is that agencies shall "propose or adopt a regulation only upon a reasoned determination that the benefits of the intended regulation justify its costs." The order also says that when setting regulatory priorities, "each agency shall consider, to the extent reasonable, the degree and nature of the risks posed by various substances or activities within its jurisdiction." The executive order's "regulatory philosophy" states that unless a statute requires another regulatory approach, "in choosing among alternative regulatory approaches, agencies should select those approaches that maximize net benefits."[90]

During the formal Executive Order 12866 review process, OIRA analyzes the draft rule in light of the principles of the executive order and discusses the rule with staff and officials at the rulemaking agency. OIRA may also discuss the draft rule with other agencies with whom interagency coordination will be necessary, and may meet or otherwise communicate with interested stakeholders outside of the federal government.[91] At the end of the review OIRA either concludes that the draft rule is consistent with the principles of the executive order (the majority of the cases) or returns the rule to the agency "for further consideration." In some cases agencies withdraw their draft rules during OIRA's review. If the draft is a proposed rule, the agency may then publish an NPRM. If the draft is a final rule, the agency may then publish a final rule and allow the rule to take effect. OIRA staff also sometimes review draft rules informally before their formal submission under the executive order—particularly when there is a statutory or legal deadline or when a rule has a large impact on society.

OIRA's formal review process has not changed substantially since Executive Order 12866 was issued in 1993.[92] However, GAO reported in September 2003 that there had been several changes in OIRA policies and practices since the current OIRA Administrator (Dr. John Graham) took office in July 2001, including (1) increased use of public letters explaining why OIRA returned rules to agencies for their consideration and suggesting regulatory action, (2) increased emphasis on cost-benefit analysis and peer review of agencies' rules, (3) stricter adherence to the 90-day time limit for OIRA review, (4) improvements in the transparency of the OIRA review process, and (5) an increase in the size and skills of OIRA's staff.[93] Underlying many of these changes is a shift in how OIRA administrators view the office's role in the rulemaking process—from "counselor" to the agencies to regulatory "gatekeeper." GAO also concluded that, certain changes notwithstanding, the OIRA review process was still not very transparent to the public, and recommended several changes in OIRA's disclosure policies.

GAO and others have also examined agencies' analyses of economically significant rules under the executive order.[94] For example, in 1998 GAO reported that some of the 20 economic analyses that it examined from five agencies did not incorporate all of the best practices set forth in OMB's guidance.[95] Five of the analyses did not discuss alternatives to the proposed regulatory action and, in many cases, it was not clear why the agencies used certain assumptions. Also, five of the analyses did not discuss uncertainty associated with the agencies' estimates of benefits and/or costs or document the agencies' reasons for not doing so.

Executive Order 12866 also includes several other notable requirements. For example, section 5 of the order requires agencies to periodically review their existing significant regulations to determine whether they should be modified or eliminated. In March 1995, President Clinton reemphasized this requirement by directing each agency to conduct a page-by-page review of all existing regulations. In June 1995, the President announced that 16,000 pages had been eliminated from the *Code of Federal Regulations*. GAO reported on this review effort in October 1997, noting that the page elimination totals that four agencies reported did not take into account pages that had been added while the eliminations took place.[96] GAO also reported that about half of the actions taken appeared to have no effect on the burden felt by regulated entities, would have little effect, or could increase regulatory burden.

Executive Order 13422

On January 18, 2007, President George W. Bush issued Executive Order 13422, making the most significant amendments to Executive Order 12866 since it was published. The changes made by this new executive order were controversial, characterized by some as a "power grab" by the White House that undermines public protections and lessens congressional authority and by others as "a paragon of common sense and good government." The most important changes made by Executive Order 13422 fell into five general categories: (1) a requirement that agencies identify in writing the specific market failure or problem that warrants a new regulation, (2) a requirement that each agency head designate a presidential appointee within the agency as a "regulatory policy officer" who can control upcoming rulemaking activity in that agency, (3) a requirement that agencies provide their best estimates of the cumulative regulatory costs and benefits of rules they expect to publish in the coming year, (4) an expansion of OIRA review to include significant guidance documents,[97] and (5) a provision permitting agencies to consider whether to use more formal rulemaking procedures in certain cases.[98]

In the first half of 2007, two House subcommittees held three oversight hearings on the order. A provision was added to the appropriations measure funding OMB for FY2008 that would have prevented the implementation of the executive order, but the measure was eliminated from the final version of the legislation. On January 30, 2009, President Barack Obama issued Executive Order 13497, which (among other things) revoked Executive Order 13422.[99] As a result, Executive Order 12866 was returned to the form when it was issued in September 1993.

Executive Order 13563

On January 18, 2011, President Obama issued Executive Order 13563 on "Improving Regulation and Regulatory Review."[100] Section 1(b) of the new order states that "This order is supplemental to and reaffirms the principles, structures, and definitions governing contemporary regulatory review that were established in Executive Order 12866 of September 30, 1993." Although similar to the 1993 order in many respects, Executive Order 13563 contains some new provisions. For example, Section 2(b) of the order states that agencies should generally provide "timely online access to the rulemaking docket on regulations.gov, including relevant scientific and technical findings, in an open format that can be easily searched and downloaded. For proposed rules, such access shall include, to the extent feasible and permitted by law, an opportunity for public comment on all pertinent parts of the rulemaking docket, including relevant scientific and technical findings."

Perhaps most notably, Section 6(b) of the new order requires agencies to initiate retrospective reviews of their existing rules. Specifically, it states,

> Within 120 days of the date of this order, each agency shall develop and submit to the Office of Information and Regulatory Affairs a preliminary plan, consistent with law and its resources and regulatory priorities, under which the agency will periodically review its existing significant regulations to determine whether any such regulations should be modified, streamlined, expanded, or repealed so as to make the agency's regulatory program more effective or less burdensome in achieving the regulatory objectives.

Section 5(a) of Executive Order 12866 had previously required agencies to submit a plan for retrospective reviews to OIRA, so this provision appears to require agencies to update those plans. On February 2, 2011, the OIRA

Administrator issued guidance to federal agencies on the implementation of the executive order, including these retrospective reviews.[101]

Other Executive Orders and Directives

Agencies other than independent regulatory agencies must also be aware of an array of other rulemaking requirements contained in executive orders and presidential directives. For example:

- Executive Order 13132 on "Federalism" requires covered federal agencies to "have an accountable process to ensure meaningful and timely input by State and local officials in the development of regulatory policies that have federalism implications."[102] The order defines "federalism implications" as "substantial direct effects on the States, on the relationship between the national government and the States, or on the distribution of power and responsibilities among the various levels of government." Federal agencies are prohibited from promulgating any regulation with unfunded federalism implications unless they have (1) consulted with state and local officials early in the development of the proposed rule, and (2) prepared a "federalism summary impact statement" consisting of a description of the prior consultation with state and local officials, a summary of their concerns and the agency's position regarding the need to issue the rule, and a statement of the extent to which the officials' concerns have been met. The order gives agencies substantial discretion regarding its implementation. For example, it does not define what type of regulatory action constitutes "substantial direct effects," and says the consultation and impact statement requirements apply "to the extent practicable."[103]
- Executive Order 12630 on constitutionally protected property rights says each agency "shall be guided by" certain principles when formulating or implementing policies that have "takings" implications.[104] For example, the order says that private property should be taken only for "real and substantial threats," and "be no greater than is necessary."[105]
- Executive Order 12889 on the North American Free Trade Agreement generally requires agencies subject to the APA to provide at least a 75-day comment period for any "proposed Federal technical

regulation or any Federal sanitary or phytosanitary measure of general application."[106]

- Executive Order 12898 on environmental justice says (among other things) that each agency must develop a strategy that identifies and addresses disproportionately high and adverse human health or environmental effects of its programs, policies, and activities on minority populations and low income populations.[107] It also says that environmental human health research should include diverse segments of the population in epidemiological and clinical studies, and that agencies should identify rules that should be revised to meet the objectives of the order.
- Executive Order 12988 on civil justice reform generally requires agencies reviewing existing and new regulations to ensure that they comply with specific requirements (e.g., "eliminate drafting errors and ambiguity" and "provide a clear legal standard for affected conduct") to improve regulatory drafting in order to minimize litigation.[108] Agencies formulating proposed regulations are directed to "make every reasonable effort" to ensure that they, among other things, specify in clear language any preemptive or retroactive effects, and the effect on existing law.
- Executive Order 13045 on protection of children from environmental health risks and safety risks says that for any substantive rulemaking action that is likely to result in an economically significant rule that concerns an environmental health risk or safety risk that may disproportionately affect children, the agency must provide OIRA with (1) an evaluation of the environmental or safety effects on children and (2) an explanation of why the planned regulation is preferable to other potentially effective and reasonably feasible alternatives.[109]
- Executive Order 13175 on consultation and coordination with Indian tribal governments generally prohibits agencies from promulgating any regulation not required by law that has tribal implications and imposes substantial direct costs on tribal governments unless the necessary funds are provided or the agency consults with tribal officials and provides a "tribal summary impact statement" describing those consultations.[110] Similar consultation and impact statement requirements apply to rules that preempt tribal laws.
- Executive Order 13211 on energy impacts requires agencies (to the extent permitted by law) to prepare and submit to OMB a "statement of energy effects" for significant energy actions.[111] The statement,

published in the NPRM and the final rule, is to include a detailed statement of "any adverse effects on energy supply, distribution, or use" for the action and reasonable alternatives and their effects.

- Executive Order 13272 on small entities generally requires federal agencies to issue (by February 2003) written procedures and policies to ensure proper consideration during the rulemaking process of the impacts of their draft rules on small entities.[112] The order also requires agencies to notify the SBA Chief Counsel for Advocacy of any draft rules that may have a significant economic impact on a substantial number of small entities, and to give "every appropriate consideration" to any comments the Chief Counsel provides.

In addition to executive orders, presidential memoranda or directives can also affect the rulemaking process. For example:

- a March 4, 1995, presidential memorandum directed federal agencies to (among other things) focus their regulatory programs on results, not process, and expand their use of negotiated rulemaking.
- an April 21, 1995, memorandum directed agencies to waive or reduce penalties in certain circumstances, and to reduce the frequency of reports the public is required to provide to the government.
- a June 1, 1998, presidential directive required agencies to use plain language in proposed and final rulemaking documents.

CONCLUSION

During the past 60 to 65 years, Congress and various Presidents have made numerous attempts to add structure, economy, efficiency, accountability, and greater public access and transparency to the regulatory process. In this regard, Congress has enacted laws such as the Administrative Procedure Act, the Regulatory Flexibility Act, the Paperwork Reduction Act, and the Unfunded Mandates Reform Act that require some type of procedure, review, and/or analysis of draft rules by the rulemaking agencies themselves or by outside parties. Presidential rulemaking requirements have often focused on coordination of agencies' regulatory efforts with the President's priorities and attempts to improve the quality of regulations through cost-benefit analysis, risk assessment analysis, and the consideration of specific factors in the rulemaking process (e.g., environmental justice, children, and property rights). Underlying many of these congressional and presidential requirements is an attempt to ensure that certain interests or issues are considered during the rulemaking process and/or to minimize the burden associated with federal regulations.

However, these rulemaking requirements impose burdens of their own on rulemaking agencies, and clearly are a factor (although it is unclear whether they are the most important factor) in the length of time it takes agencies to issue rules. Federal agencies must be aware of the cross-cutting and the program-specific statutory and executive requirements underlying their regulations and must craft rules that are consistent with those requirements—or run the risk of having their rules returned to them by OIRA or rejected by Congress or the courts. Several of these statutes and orders indicate that their requirements may be integrated with or satisfied by the requirements in other statutes or orders. For example, the Regulatory Flexibility Act states that federal agencies can develop their regulatory agendas and perform their regulatory flexibility analyses "in conjunction with or as a part of any other agenda or analysis required by any other law." Some observers believe that integration and consolidation of all these requirements could improve the rulemaking process. In 1993 the Administrative Conference of the United States noted that the simple requirements in the Administrative Procedure Act for informal rulemaking had been "overlain with an increasing number of constraints," including those imposed by Congress, Presidents, and the courts. The Administrative Conference recommended a "coordinated framework of proposals aimed at promoting efficient and effective rulemaking." Since then, the number of rulemaking requirements has increased.

On the other hand, many of these statutory and executive order provisions provide the agencies substantial discretion regarding when and how the rulemaking requirements are to be applied. For example, because the Regulatory Flexibility Act does not define the term "significant impact on a substantial number of small entities," agencies have a great deal of latitude to determine when a regulatory flexibility analysis is required. Similarly, Executive Order 13132 does not define the term "significant federalism implications," so agencies have substantial discretion in deciding whether the analytical requirements of the order have been triggered. Other rulemaking requirements are written in such a way that they actually apply to only a small number of rules. For example, title II of the Unfunded Mandates Reform Act does not apply to any rules published by independent regulatory agencies or any rules for which an agency determines there is "good cause" not to publish a notice of proposed rulemaking. Other rules are exempt from UMRA if they are conditions of federal financial assistance or enforce constitutional rights.

The discretion and exceptions built into these rulemaking statutes and orders diminish their impact, and allow agencies knowledgeable of their provisions to avoid many of the analyses and procedures they seem to require. For example, on hundreds of occasions, agencies have stated in the preambles to their rules that because they believed there was "good cause" not to issue a notice of proposed rulemaking, the requirements of the RFA and/or UMRA do not apply. Agencies also have standard language that they insert into preambles certifying that their rules do not require regulatory flexibility analyses or UMRA written statements. And if agencies are not required to prepare regulatory flexibility analyses for their proposed rules, they are also exempt from the SBREFA requirements to prepare small entity compliance guides and (in the case of OSHA, EPA, and CFPB) to convene advocacy review panels.

Because of the inevitability of regulation and its associated burden, efforts to either tighten existing requirements or impose new ones are likely to continue.

A clear understanding of the existing requirements and how they have been implemented may inform any such future efforts.

For Additional Information

Kerwin, Cornelius M., Rulemaking: How Government Agencies Write Law and Make Policy, Third Edition (Washington: CQ Press, 2003).

Lubbers, Jeffrey S., ed., A Guide To Federal Agency Rulemaking, Fourth Edition (Chicago: ABA Publishing, 2006).

In addition, information regarding a variety of regulatory issues is available at the following websites:

Center for Progressive Regulation
http://www.progressiveregulation.org

Center for Regulatory Effectiveness
http://www.thecre.com

Competitive Enterprise Institute
http://www.cei.org

Government Accountability Office
(GAO, formerly the General Accounting Office)
http://www.gao.gov

Government Printing Office (GPO)
http://www.gpoaccess.gov/nara/index.html

Office of Management and Budget
http://www.whitehouse.gov/omb

OMB Watch
http://www.ombwatch.org

Regulations.gov
http://www.regulations.gov

Regulatory Information Service Center
http://www.reginfo.gov

End Notes

[1] Colin Diver, "Regulatory Precision," in Keith Hawkins and John Thomas, eds., Making Regulatory Policy (Pittsburgh: University of Pittsburgh Press, 1989), p. 199.

[2] Cornelius M. Kerwin, Rulemaking: How Government Agencies Write Law and Make Public Policy, 2nd ed., (Washington: CQ Press, 1999), p. ix.

[3] 5 U.S.C. §551 (4).

[4] As used in this report, the term "independent regulatory agencies" refers to the boards and commissions identified as such in the Paperwork Reduction Act (44 U.S.C. §3502(5)), including the Federal Communications Commission, the Federal Energy Regulatory Commission, the Nuclear Regulatory Commission, and the Securities and Exchange Commission. The term "independent agencies" refers to other agencies that answer directly to the President, but are not part of Cabinet departments.

[5] See, for example, Thomas O. McGarity, "Some Thoughts on 'Deossifying' the Rulemaking Process, Duke Law Journal, vol. 41 (June 1992), pp. 1385-1462; Richard J. Pierce, Jr., "Seven Ways to Deossify Agency Rulemaking," 47 Administrative Law Review, vol. 47, winter 1995, pp. 59-93; Paul R. Verkuil, "Rulemaking Ossification—A Modest Proposal," Administrative Law Review, vol. 47 (summer 1995), pp. 453-459.

[6] National Advisory Committee on Occupational Safety and Health, Report and Recommendations Related to OSHA's Standards Development Process (Washington: June 6, 2000).

[7] For example, 29 U.S.C. §1306(a)(3)(A) states that the annual premium rate payable in the case of a single-employer plan for basic benefits is "an amount equal to the sum of $19 plus the additional premium (if any) determined under subparagraph (E) for each individual who is a participant in such plan during the plan year."

[8] DOT's 1998 appropriations act stated that "(n)one of the funds in this Act shall be available to prepare, propose, or promulgate any regulations ... in any model year that differs from the standards promulgated for such automobiles prior to the enactment of this section."

[9] For an examination of the amount of regulatory discretion afforded in specific statutes, see U.S. General Accounting Office, Regulatory Burden: Some Agencies' Claims Regarding Lack of Rulemaking Discretion Have Merit, GAO/GGD-99-20, Jan. 8, 1999.

[10] For more information on PPACA rulemaking provisions, see CRS Report R41180, Rulemaking Requirements and Authorities in the Patient Protection and Affordable Care Act (PPACA), by Curtis W. Copeland.

[11] Industrial Union Department v. American Petroleum Institute, 448 U.S. 607 (1980).

[12] See, for example, American Textile Mfrs. Inst., Inc. v. Donovan, 452 U.S. 490 (1981) and United Steelworkers v. Marshall, 647 F.2d 1189 (D.C. Cir. 1980), cert. denied, 453 U.S. 913 (1981).

[13] See, for example, Motor Vehicle Manufacturers Association v State Farm Mutual Automobile Insurance Co., 463 U.S. 29 (1983). The Supreme Court said the agency "must examine the relevant data and articulate a satisfactory explanation of its action, including a 'rational connection between the facts found and the choice made.'"

[14] 1 C.F.R. ch. I, pts. 1-22.

[15] Electronic access to the Federal Register is provided through a Government Printing Office website at http://www.gpoaccess.gov/fr/index.html.

[16] For more on formal and other types of rulemaking, as well as information on judicial review, see CRS Report R41546, A Brief Overview of Rulemaking and Judicial Review, by Vanessa K. Burrows and Todd Garvey.

[17] Some agencies begin the rulemaking process by publishing an "advance notice of proposed rulemaking in which the agency notifies the public that it is considering an area for rulemaking and often requests comments on the appropriate scope or topics of the rule. The APA does not require the use of advance notices, but some other statutes require it for particular types of rules. Similarly, agencies may issue a "supplemental notice of proposed rulemaking" after an NPRM is issued if they wish to obtain public comment on new factual proposals before issuing a final rule.

[18] Executive Order 12866, discussed in detail later in this report, suggests that agencies allow the public at least 60 days to comment for "significant" rules.

[19] The APA judicial review provisions are codified at 5 U.S.C 701-706. For more information on the APA and judicial review, see CRS Report R41546, A Brief Overview of Rulemaking and Judicial Review, by Vanessa K. Burrows and Todd Garvey.

[20] In addition to the APA exceptions, Congress sometimes includes specific exemptions from notice and comment procedures in other statutes. For example, section 161(d) under title I of the Federal Agriculture Improvement and Reform Act of 1996 (P.L. 104-127, 110 Stat. 934-935) instructed the Secretary of Agriculture and the Commodity Credit Corporation to issue regulations not later than 90 days after the date of enactment of the title, without regard to the notice and comment provisions of the APA.

[21] Senate Committee on the Judiciary, "Administrative Procedure Act: Legislative History," Senate Document 248, 79th Congress, 2nd Session (1946).

[22] For discussions of these court cases, see Ellen R. Jordan, "The Administrative Procedure Act's 'Good Cause' Exemption," Administrative Law Review, 36, spring 1984, pp. 113-178; and Catherine J. Lanctot, "The Good Cause Exception: Danger to Notice and Comment Requirements Under the Administrative Procedure Act," Georgetown Law Journal, 68 (Feb. 1980), pp. 765-782.

[23] See American Federation of Government Employees, AFL-CIO v. Block, 655 F.2d 1153, 1156 (D.C. Cir 1981); and Mobay Chemical Corp. v. Gorsuch, (682 F.2d 419, 426 (3rd Cir.), cert. denied, 459 U.S. 988 (1982). In another case (Action on Smoking and Health v. CAB, 713 F.2d 795, 800 [D.C. Cir 1983]), the court said that allowing broad use of the good cause exception would "carve the heart out of the statute."

[24] For more, see Ronald M. Levin, "More on Direct Final Rulemaking: Streamlining, Not Corner Cutting," Administrative Law Review, 51 (summer 1999), pp. 757-766.

[25] See Office of the Vice President, Improving Regulatory Systems: Accompanying Report of the National Performance Review (Washington: Sept. 1993). The Administrative Conference was established by statute as an independent agency to promote improvements in the efficiency, adequacy, and fairness of procedures by which federal agencies conduct regulatory programs, administer grants and benefits, and perform related governmental functions.

[26] For more, see Michael Asimow, "Interim Final Rules: Making Haste Slowly," Administrative Law Review, 51 (summer 1999), pp. 703-755.

[27] U.S. General Accounting Office, Federal Rulemaking: Agencies Often Published Final Actions Without Proposed Rules, GAO/GGD-98-126, Aug. 31, 1998.

[28] See Juan J. Lavilla, "The Good Cause Exemption to Notice and Comment Rulemaking Requirements Under the Administrative Procedure Act," The Administrative Law Journal, 3 (fall 1989), pp. 317-423 for another study on the use of the good cause exception.

[29] NEPA regulations are codified at 40 CFR Parts 1500-1508.

[30] NEPA Task Force, Report to the Council on Environmental Quality, Modernizing NEPA Implementation (Washington: Sept. 2003).

[31] For more information this legislation and on NEPA, see CRS Report RL33152, The National Environmental Policy Act (NEPA): Background and Implementation, by Linda Luther.

[32] For example, EPA's Toxics Release Inventory (TRI) program is essentially a database created through collections of information imposed on businesses to inform the public about chemical hazards in their communities. TRI reports require businesses in certain industries to report the quantity of any of more than 600 chemicals entering each environmental medium on site, transfers of the chemical in wastes to off-site locations, on-site treatment methods and efficiency, and source reduction and recycling activities.

[33] For an up-to-date inventory of OMB-approved information collections, see http://www.reginfo.gov/public/do/ PRAMain.

[34] Independent regulatory agencies can, by majority vote, void any OIRA disapproval of a proposed collection of information.

[35] An agency's annual paperwork burden-hour estimate is a function of (1) the frequency of the information collection, (2) the estimated number of respondents, and (3) amount of time that the agency estimates it takes each respondent to complete the collection. For example, if an agency estimates that an information collection conducted twice each year will take each of the estimated 10,000 respondents 10 hours to complete each time, the total annual burden hour estimate for the collection is 200,000 burden hours (2 times 10,000 times 10).

[36] The act's definition of an agency excludes only the General Accounting Office, the Federal Election Commission, the governments of the District of Columbia, U.S. territories and possessions, and government-owned contractor-operated facilities.

[37] OMB is required to report to Congress on the implementation of the PRA, and does so through an annual "information collection budget." For the 2010 report, see http://www.whitehouse.gov/sites/default/files/omb/inforeg/ icb/icb_2010.pdf.

[38] For more information on the PRA, see CRS Report R40636, Paperwork Reduction Act (PRA): OMB and Agency Responsibilities and Burden Estimates, by Curtis W. Copeland and Vanessa K. Burrows.

[39] See http://www.reginfo.gov/public/do/PRAMain for information collection totals.

[40] Many agencies are apparently aware of this limitation; GAO estimated that in more than 500 final rules published in 1997 the agencies specifically stated that the RFA was not applicable or that a regulatory flexibility analysis was not required because the action was not preceded by an NPRM. See GAO/GGD-98-126, p. 31.

[41] U.S. Small Business Administration, 20 Years of the Regulatory Flexibility Act: Rulemaking in a Dynamic Economy (Washington: 2000).

[42] This requirement, as well as a similar requirement in Executive Order 12866, is generally met via entries in the Unified Agenda of Federal Regulatory and Deregulatory Actions. The Unified Agenda is published twice each year in the Federal Register by the Regulatory Information Service Center, and provides uniform reporting of data on regulatory activities under development throughout the federal government.

[43] For an examination of the first five advocacy review panels were implemented, see U.S. General Accounting Office, Regulatory Reform: Implementation of the Small Business Advocacy Review Panel Requirements, GAO/GGD-98-36, March 18, 1996.

[44] U.S. General Accounting Office, Regulatory Flexibility Act: Inherent Weaknesses May Limit Its Usefulness for Small Governments, GAO/HRD-91-16, Jan. 11, 1991.

[45] U.S. General Accounting Office, Regulatory Flexibility Act: Status of Agencies' Compliance, GAO/GGD-94-105, Apr. 27, 1994.

[46] U.S. General Accounting Office, Regulatory Flexibility Act: Agencies' Interpretations of Review Requirements Vary, GAO/GGD-99-55, Apr. 2, 1999; U.S. General Accounting Office, Regulatory Flexibility Act: Implementation in EPA Program Offices and Proposed Lead Rule, GAO/GGD-00-193. Sept. 20, 2000.

[47] U.S. General Accounting Office, Regulatory Flexibility Act: Key Terms Still Need to Be Clarified, GAO-01-669T, Apr. 24, 2001.

[48] For more information about the RFA, see CRS Report RL34355, The Regulatory Flexibility Act: Implementation Issues and Proposed Reforms, by Curtis W. Copeland.

[49] U.S. General Accounting Office, Regulatory Reform: Compliance Guide Requirement Has Had Little Effect on Agency Practices, GAO-02-172, Dec. 28, 2001.

[50] In 2007, Congress enacted some changes to these requirements. See P.L. 110-28, Title VI, Subtitle B, sec. 7005. Among other things, agencies must prepare compliance guides for any rule for which it must prepare a final regulatory flexibility analysis, and must post the guides on their websites.

[51] U.S. General Accounting Office, Regulatory Reform: Implementation of Selected Agencies' Civil Penalty Relief Policies for Small Entities, GAO-01-280, Feb. 20, 2001.

[52] For a detailed discussion of CRA procedures, see CRS Report RL31160, Disapproval of Regulations by Congress: Procedure Under the Congressional Review Act, by Richard S. Beth.

[53] Nevertheless, some rules have not been submitted. See CRS Report R40997, Congressional Review Act: Rules Not Submitted to GAO and Congress, by Curtis W. Copeland.

[54] To view these reports, see http://www.gao.gov/decisions/majrule/majrule.php.

[55] A related CRS analysis of the implementation of the CRA describes several possible impediments to the law's use. See CRS Report RL30116, Congressional Review of Agency Rulemaking: An Update and Assessment of The Congressional Review Act after a Decade, by Morton Rosenberg. See also Morton Rosenberg, "Whatever Happened to Congressional Review of Agency Rulemaking?: A Brief Overview, Assessment, and Proposal for Reform," Administrative Law Review, vol. 51, fall 1999, pp. 1051-1092.

[56] See, for example, Susan E. Dudley, "Reversing Midnight Regulations," Regulation, vol. 24 (Spring 2001), p. 9, who noted that the "veto threat is diminished [after a transition], since the president whose administration issued the regulations is no longer in office." For a discussion of which rules may be carried over and disapproved after a transition, see CRS Report RL34633, Congressional Review Act: Disapproval of Rules in a Subsequent Session of Congress, by Curtis W. Copeland and Richard S. Beth.

[57] For more information, see CRS Report RL34354, Congressional Influence on Rulemaking and Regulation Through Appropriations Restrictions, by Curtis W. Copeland.

[58] For an overview of UMRA, see CRS Report R40957, Unfunded Mandates Reform Act: History, Impact, and Issues, by Robert Jay Dilger and Richard S. Beth.

[59] In recent years, OIRA's annual report on UMRA has been combined with its report on the costs and benefits of federal regulations. See, for example, Office of Management and Budget, Office of Information and Regulatory Affairs, 2010 Report to Congress on the Benefits and Costs of Federal Regulations and Unfunded Mandates on State, Local, and Tribal Entities, available at http://www.whitehouse.gov/sites/default/files/omb/ legislative/ reports/ 2010_Benefit_Cost_Report.pdf.

[60] U.S. General Accounting Office, Unfunded Mandates: Reform Act Has Had Little Effect on Agencies' Rulemaking Actions, GAO/GGD-98-30, Feb. 4, 1998.

[61] U.S. General Accounting Office, Unfunded Mandates: Analysis of Reform Act Coverage, GAO-04-637, May 12, 2004.

[62] U.S. Government Accountability Office, Unfunded Mandates: Views Vary About Reform Act's Strengths, Weaknesses, and Options for Improvement, GAO-05-454, March 31, 2005.

[63] Testimony of Denise M. Fantone, Director, Strategic Issues, U.S. Government Accountability Office, before the Subcommittee on Technology, Information Policy, Intergovernmental Relations and Procurement Reform, House Committee on Oversight of Government Management, available at http://www.gao.gov/products/GAO-11-385T.

[64] OMB published those government-wide guidelines in interim form on September 28, 2001, and in updated final form on February 22, 2002. See Office of Management and Budget, "Guidelines for Ensuring and Maximizing the Quality, Objectivity, Utility, and Integrity of Information Disseminated by Federal Agencies; Republication," Federal Register, vol. 67, no. 36, Feb. 22, 2002, p. 8452.

[65] For a copy of this report, see http://www.whitehouse.gov/omb/inforeg/fy03_info_quality_ rpt.pdf.

[66] For a copy of this report, see http://www.ombwatch.org/infor/dataqualityreport.pdr.

[67] Salt Institute; Chamber of Commerce of the United States of America v. Michael O. Leavitt, Secretary of Health and Human Services, No. 05-1097, Mar. 6, 2006.

[68] In re: Operation of the Missouri River Sys. Litig., No. 03-MD-1555 at 49 (D. Minn. June 21, 2004) (order granting motions for summary judgment); and Salt Institute and the Chamber of Commerce of the United States of America v. Tommy G. Thompson, Secretary, U.S.

Department of Health and Human Services, Civil Action No. 04-359, Nov. 15, 2004. In the Salt Institute case, the court ruled that there is no private right of action under the IQA, saying that the "language in the IQA reflects Congress's intent that any challenges to the quality of information disseminated by federal agencies should take place in administrative proceedings before federal agencies and not the courts." The court also said that judicial review under the APA was not available because the agency's actions did not constitute a "final agency action," and because the agency decisions were within the discretion provided to the agency by law.

[69] For more information on the IQA, see CRS Report RL32532, The Information Quality Act: OMB's Guidance and Initial Implementation, by Curtis W. Copeland.

[70] Office of Management and Budget, Executive Office of the President, "Proposed Bulletin on Peer Review and Information Quality," Federal Register, vol. 68, no. 178, Sept. 15, 2003, p. 54023.

[71] For a copy of the revised peer review bulletin, see http://www.whitehouse.gov/omb/inforeg/peer_review041404.pdf. For a summary of the public and agency comments provided regarding the first bulletin, see http://www.whitehouse.gov/omb/inforeg/peer_review_comment.pdf. Copies of the comments can be viewed at http://www.whitehouse.gov/omb/inforeg/2003iq/iq_list.html.

[72] Office of Management and Budget, Final Information Quality Bulletin for Peer Review, Dec. 15, 2004, available at http://www.whitehouse.gov/omb/inforeg/peer2004/peer_bulletin.pdf.

[73] Office of Management and Budget, Final Information Quality Bulletin for Peer Review, 70 Federal Register 2664 (Jan. 14, 2005).

[74] In a Sept. 20, 2001, memorandum to the President's Management Council, the OIRA Administrator previously indicated that, during its reviews of agencies' draft rules under Executive Order 12866, it would give a "measure of deference" to regulatory analyses that had been peer reviewed.

[75] For more information, see CRS Report RL32680, Peer Review: OMB's Proposed, Revised, and Final Bulletins, by Curtis W. Copeland and Eric A. Fischer.

[76] For more information, see CRS Report R40520, Federal Advisory Committees: An Overview, by Wendy R. Ginsberg.

[77] For a complete discussion of negotiated rulemaking, see Administrative Conference of the United States, Negotiated Rulemaking Sourcebook (Sept. 1995).

[78] Cary Coglianese, "Assessing Consensus: The Promise and Performance of Negotiated Rulemaking," Duke University Law Journal, vol. 46 (1997), pp. 1255-1349.

[79] Laura I. Langbein and Cornelius M. Kerwin, "Regulatory Negotiation versus Conventional Rulemaking: Claims, Counterclaims, and Empirical Evidence," Journal of Public Administration Research and Theory, vol. 10 (2000), pp. 599-632.

[80] For more information, see CRS Report RL32452, Negotiated Rulemaking, by Curtis W. Copeland.

[81] For a discussion of federal policies relating to certification and consensus standards, see U.S. General Accounting Office, Certification Requirements: New Guidance Should Encourage Transparency in Agency Decisionmaking, GAO/GGD-99-170, Sept. 24, 1999.

[82] The accounting statement requirement had been included in appropriations bills for several previous years on a year-to-year basis.

[83] See http://www.whitehouse.gov/omb/inforeg_regpol_reports_congress/ for a compilation of these reports.

[84] For a comparison of the Regulations.gov website with individual agency systems, see U.S. General Accounting Office, Electronic Rulemaking: Efforts to Facilitate Public Participation Can Be Improved, GAO-03-90, Sept. 17, 2003.

[85] For more information, see CRS Report RL34210, Electronic Rulemaking in the Federal Government, by Curtis W. Copeland.

[86] These lists of compliance assistance resources are available on the OMB website at http://www.whitehouse.gov/omb/ inforeg/infocoll.html#sbpra and on the SBA website at http://www.sba.gov/ombudsman/compliance/ complianceassist.html.

[87] Executive Order 12866, "Regulatory Planning and Review," 58 Federal Register 51735, Oct. 4, 1993.

[88] Although issued on September 30, 1993, the executive order was not printed in the Federal Register until several days later. See The President, "Executive Order 12866—Regulatory Planning and Review," Federal Register, vol. 58, no. 190 (Oct. 4, 1993).

[89] For a current list of regulations under OIRA review or reviews completed within the past 30 days, see http://www.whitehouse.gov/omb/inforeg/regpol-regs_under12866.html.

[90] In January 1996, OIRA published a document that described "best practices" for preparing the economic analyses called for by the executive order. This document was revised and issued as guidance in 2000. In September 2003, OMB and the Council of Economic Advisors finalized new guidance for agencies on regulatory analysis, refining and replacing the 1996 "best practices" document. For a copy of this guidance, see http://www.whitehouse. gov/omb/ circulars/a004/a-4.pdf.

[91] OIRA has indicated that it will try and accommodate any request for a meeting with parties outside of the federal government. OIRA discloses these contacts on its website at http://www.whitehouse.gov/omb/oira/meetings.html. A representative from the agency issuing the rule must be invited to any such meeting.

[92] Executive Order 13258 reassigned certain responsibilities from the Vice President to the President's chief of staff, but otherwise did not change the OIRA review process. See The President, "Executive Order 13258—Amending Executive Order 12866 on Regulatory Planning and Review," Federal Register, vol. 67, no. 40, Feb. 28, 2002, p. 9385.

[93] U.S. General Accounting Office, Rulemaking: OMB's Role in Reviews of Agencies' Draft Rules and the Transparency of Those Reviews, GAO-03-929, Sept. 22, 2003.

[94] See, for example, Richard D. Morgenstern, ed., Economic Analyses at EPA: Assessing Regulatory Impact (Washington: Resources for the Future, 1997); and Robert W. Hahn, ed., Risks, Costs, and Lives Saved: Getting Better Results from Regulation (Washington: AEI Press, 1996).

[95] U.S. General Accounting Office, Regulatory Reform: Agencies Could Improve Development, Documentation, and Clarity of Regulatory Economic Analyses, GAO/RCED-98-142, May 26, 1998.

[96] U.S. General Accounting Office, Regulatory Reform: Agencies' Efforts to Eliminate and Revise Rules Yield Mixed Results, GAO/GGD-98-3, Oct. 2, 1997.

[97] On the same day that E.O. 13422 was issued, OMB also issued a "Final Bulletin for Agency Good Guidance Practices" that mirrored, in many respects, the provisions in this section of the executive order. Unlike the order, however, the bulletin requires agencies to include certain standard elements in their significant guidance documents, to list those documents on the agencies' websites, and to publish a notice in the Federal Register soliciting public comments on economically significant documents. To view a copy of this bulletin, see http://www.whitehouse.gov/ omb/memoranda/fy2007/m07-07.pdf; and Office of

Management and Budget, "Final Bulletin for Agency Good Guidance Practices," 72 Federal Register 3432, January 25, 2007.

[98] For more information, see CRS Report RL33862, Changes to the OMB Regulatory Review Process by Executive Order 13422, by Curtis W. Copeland.

[99] Executive Order 13497, "Revocation of Certain Executive Orders Concerning Regulatory Planning and Review," 74 Federal Register 6113, February 4, 2009.

[100] Executive Order 13563, "Improving Regulation and Regulatory Review," 76 Federal Register 3821, January 21, 2011.

[101] See http://www.whitehouse.gov/sites/default/files/omb/memoranda/2011/m11-10.pdf.

[102] Executive Order 13132, "Federalism," 64 Federal Register 43255, Aug. 10, 1999.

[103] Executive Order 12612, the previous executive order on federalism, also gave federal agencies broad discretion to determine the applicability of its requirements. GAO examined the implementation of this order and concluded that its analytical requirements were rarely implemented. See U.S. General Accounting Office, Federalism: Previous Initiatives Have Had Little Effect on Agency Rulemaking, GAO/T-GGD-99-3, June 30, 1999.

[104] Executive Order 12630, "Governmental Actions and Interference with Constitutionally Protected Property Rights," 53 Federal Register 8859, Mar. 18, 1988.

[105] For an analysis of how this executive order has been implemented, see U.S. General Accounting Office, Regulatory Takings: Implementation of Executive Order on Government Actions Affecting Private Property Use, GAO-03-1015, Sept. 19, 2003.

[106] Executive Order 12889, "Implementation of the North American Free Trade Agreement," 58 Federal Register 69681, Dec. 30, 1993.

[107] Executive Order 12898, "Federal Actions to Address Environmental Justice in Minority Populations and Low-Income Populations," 59 Federal Register 7629, Feb. 16, 1994.

[108] Executive Order 12988, "Civil Justice Reform," 61 Federal Register 4729, Feb. 7, 1996.

[109] Executive Order 13045, "Protection of Children from Environmental Health Risks and Safety Risks," 62 Federal Register 19885, Apr. 23, 1997.

[110] Executive Order 13175, "Consultation and Coordination with Indian Tribal Governments," 65 Federal Register 67249, Nov. 9, 2000.

[111] Executive Order 13211, "Actions Concerning Regulations That Significantly Affect Energy Supply, Distribution, or Use," 66 Federal Register 28355, May 22, 2001.

[112] Executive Order 13272, "Proper Consideration of Small Entities in Agency Rulemaking," 67 Federal Register 53461, Aug. 16, 2002.

INDEX

C

D

E

F